THE CHRISTIAN
AND THE WORLD
readings in theology

Also in this series:
THE CHURCH: *readings in theology*
THE WORD: *readings in theology*

THE CHRISTIAN AND THE WORLD

readings in theology

ALFONS AUER
KARL RAHNER, S.J.
JOHANNES B. METZ
HEINRICH SCHLIER

WALTER DÜRIG
LEO SCHEFFCZYK
M.-D. CHENU, O.P.
HEINZ ROBERT SCHLETTE

Foreword by JOHN J. WRIGHT
Compiled at THE CANISIANUM, INNSBRUCK

P. J. Kenedy & Sons   •   New York

Nihil obstat: GALL HIGGINS, O.F.M., Cap.
          Censor Librorum
Imprimatur: TERENCE J. COOKE, V.G.
          Archdiocese of New York
New York, June 11, 1965

> *The nihil obstat and imprimatur are official declarations that a book or pamphlet is free of doctrinal or moral error. No implication is contained therein that those who have granted the nihil obstat and imprimatur agree with the contents, opinions or statements expressed.*

Library of Congress Catalog Card Number: 65–22645
Copyright © 1965 by P. J. Kenedy & Sons, New York

PRINTED IN THE UNITED STATES OF AMERICA

To our Regens,
Father Franz Braunshofer, S.J.

When I shall be dead, tell the kingdom of the earth that I have loved it much more than I ever dared to say.
—Georges Bernanos

In the name of our faith, we have the right and duty to become passionate about the things of the earth.
—Pierre Teilhard de Chardin

Foreword

THE PREVIOUS VOLUMES in this unusually solid series of theological papers have been ambitious in their editorial purpose, timely in their content, impressive in their potential contribution to the thought of our times. Its very title suggests that the present volume is their worthy successor on the first two points; the quality of its scholarship and the persuasive spirit of its presentations give it perhaps even greater promise with respect to the third.

Pilgrims and strangers on the face of the earth, constantly under the warning of St. Paul: *Nolite conformari huic saeculo,* Christians might be expected inevitably to be ill at ease in a world the beauty, truth and goodness of which, however contingent and derived, powerfully invite not only the inquiring mind and avid affections, but also a certain cult from the creatures who, though bound for eternity, know themselves to be bound up with both time and the world.

The eschatological dimension of Catholic theology—a dimension notably developed in these essays—keeps all *mystique de la terre* in the thoughtful Christian from becoming (or remaining) any mere mystique *huius saeculi*. It does not, on that account, deny the validity of the truth in things created, nor blind us to their beauty, nor leave us insensible or indifferent to their good. On the contrary, quite apart from the eternal moral significance that created goods acquire precisely from the relationship of their use to the perfection here below and the salvation hereafter of God's people, these goods have an entitive status of their own, deriving from the relationship of their ontological attributes to those of their Creator. Hence the pertinence of the tag line from Bernanos chosen by the editors to hint at the ascetical requirements following from the doctrinal reflections brought together in their book: *When I shall be dead, tell the kingdom of the earth that I have loved it much more than I ever dared to say.*

Bernanos' wistful passion recalls Robert Frost's oft-quoted *I had a lover's quarrel with the world.* In the case of the convinced Christian, the origins and predictable patterns of the "quarrel" are those implicit in the dogmatic premises and moral corollaries of that spiritual passion for the world which permeates most of these pages. The source of the lover's passion for creation particular to the Christian is in the God who so loved the world as to give His only-begotten Son, that whosoever believeth in Him may not perish, but have life everlasting (John 3:16).

The Christian's just and proper love for the world is, then, a logical as well as psychological consequence of the contemplation of the truths essential to the Incarnation. An incarnational theology—and such every authentically Catholic theology must be—can only lead to loving embrace of all that God has made and Himself has loved. This book is contemporary incarnational theology at its erudite and persuasive best.

Such theology demands of the Christian believer no mere "acceptance" of the universe, such as that reluctantly yielded in the absurd announcement by Margaret Fuller that she had decided to "accept the universe," a choice which elicited Carlyle's caustic "By God, she'd better!"

But, for all its passion (because of it?), Catholic theology *does* have its "lover's quarrel" with the world that it so gladly bids the Christian to embrace. It knows the need of a saving detachment and its love is disciplined, as fruitful love must ever be. And so, though contemporary in its preoccupations and its thrust, the theology of the present book is in the broad tradition of the *Epistle to Diognetus* with its classic statement of the Christian intellectual's balanced understanding of his role in a world which has so many and such valid claims on his affections and service, but which his integral knowledge and total love must always transcend.

The consequent "terrible tension of the devout," a tension in fact essential to the true harmony among the values of nature and grace cherished by those who love God as Creator and Redeemer of all things, derives from truths, rational and revealed, confidently faced and competently set forth by these theologians who take the Incarnation seriously. They do so because they perceive the Incarnation to be not only the pledge of their salvation and that of mankind, but also the premise of the culture they would help modern Christians to nurture. Hence the enthusiastic *yes* that they invite their students and readers to give to everything that is ours, if only we be Christ's as Christ is God's.

✠ JOHN J. WRIGHT
Bishop of Pittsburgh

Editors' Preface

IN AUGUST, 1964, the World Council of Churches chose as the first of its main study topics for the next few years the question of the church and the world. Along with Vatican II, this is yet another clear recognition on the part of all Christians of a problem special to our century: What does the phenomenon of the changing world mean for the Christian, the Church, religion?

Does secularism, which is a large aspect of the changing world, and the self-sufficient bent of the world open up to the Christian new possibilities for a greater experience of God in the world? Or does it hinder this experience, making it imperative for the Christian to react in a militant way? Does a world which is coming ever more into its own necessarily mean a proportionate decrease of the dominion of Christ over the world? Or is the "new world" finally becoming the true partner God wanted it to be?

Whatever the answers to these questions might be—and we make no claim to give the final ones here—the problem demands frank discussion, openness and a search for a constantly new outlook. They are questions from which the Christian cannot shrink, for it is in this world that he must live and experience Christ. They are questions which cannot be met by repeating time-worn solutions and outdated answers, for the new questions demand new answers, or at least newly formulated ones.

It is hoped that this book will provide at least a few guidelines for giving Christian witness in a changing world. If it helps promote an awareness of all that our faith implies in the actual world situation in which we live, it will have served its purpose.

For their encouragement and permission to prepare this book we wish to thank our Rector, Father Walter Croce, S.J., and our Regens, Father Franz Braunshofer, S.J. We wish also to thank the many professors and students here at the Canisianum without whose assistance this book could never have been brought to completion.

THE EDITORS

Canisianum, Innsbruck
On the Feast of St. Peter Canisius
April 27, 1965

Contents

Foreword	John J. Wright	ix
Editors' Preface		xiii
Acknowledgments		xvii
The authors		xix

PART ONE
THE CHRISTIAN LOOKS AT THE WORLD

The Changing Character of the Christian Understanding of the World	Alfons Auer	3
World History and Salvation History	Karl Rahner, S.J.	45
A Believer's Look at the World	Johannes B. Metz	68

PART TWO
THE CHRISTIAN EXPERIENCES CHRIST IN THE WORLD

The Dominion of Christ	Heinrich Schlier	103
The Eucharist as Symbol of the Consecration of the World	Walter Dürig	120
The Meaning of Christ's Parousia for the Salvation of Man and the Cosmos	Leo Scheffczyk	130

PART THREE
THE CHRISTIAN LIVES IN THE WORLD

Consecratio Mundi	M.-D. Chenu, O.P.	161
The Christian's Responsibility for Freedom	Heinz Robert Schlette	178
Christianity and the "New Man"	Karl Rahner, S.J.	206

EDITORS

Mauricio Ferro-Calvo   James Keethers
Charles W. Gusmer   Robert Pawson

TRANSLATORS

Charles W. Gusmer: "The Changing Character of the Christian Understanding of the World" by Alfons Auer
Karl-H. Kruger: "World History and Salvation History" by Karl Rahner, S.J.
Henry Wansbrough, O.S.B.: "A Believer's Look at the World" by Johannes B. Metz
Theodore Osbahr: "The Dominion of Christ" by Heinrich Schlier
Leo Connolly: "The Eucharist as Symbol of the Consecration of the World" by Walter Dürig
Robert Kress: "The Meaning of Christ's Parousia for the Salvation of Man and the Cosmos" by Leo Scheffczyk
George P. Alcser: "*Consecratio Mundi*" by M.-D. Chenu, O.P.
Robert Pawson: "The Christian's Responsibility for Freedom" by Heinz Robert Schlette
Karl-H. Kruger: "Christianity and the 'New Man'" by Karl Rahner, S.J.

Acknowledgments

The editors extend their thanks to the authors and publishers who gave permission to republish in this book, in translation, the following articles:

Alfons Auer: "Gestaltwandel des christlichen Weltverständnisses," *Gott in Welt I.* Freiburg-Breisgau: Herder, 1964.

Karl Rahner, S.J.: "Weltgeschichte und Heilsgeschichte" and "Das Christentum und der neue Mensch," *Schriften zur Theologie V.* Einsiedeln: Benziger Verlag, 1962. This book is being published in English by Helicon Press, Baltimore, as *Theological Investigations*, Volume V. The articles "World History and Salvation History" and "Christianity and the 'New Man'" are presented here by special arrangement with Helicon Press.

Johannes B. Metz: "Weltverständnis im Glauben," *Geist und Leben* 35 (1962), pp. 165-84.

Heinrich Schlier: "Über die Herrschaft Christi," *Geist und Leben* 30 (1957), pp. 246-56.

Walter Dürig: "Die Eucharistie als Sinn-Bild der Consecratio Mundi," *Münchener Theologische Zeitschrift* 10 (1959), pp. 283-89.

Leo Scheffczyk: "Die Wiederkunft Christi in ihrer Heilsbedeutung für die Menschheit und den Kosmos," *Lebendiges Zeugnis* 1963, Heft 1, pp. 66-87.

M.-D. Chenu, O.P.: "Consecratio Mundi," *Nouvelle Revue Théologique* 86 (1964), pp. 608-18.

Heinz Robert Schlette: "Die Verantwortung des Christen für die Freiheit," *Hochland* 54 (1961/62), pp. 293-311.

The Authors

ALFONS AUER is professor of moral theology at the University of Würzburg. In his frequent radio talks and many books, he has focused on lay spirituality, marriage problems, and the Christocentric basis of moral theology. His books include *Der Weltoffener Christ* (soon to appear in English) and *Theologie des Berufs und der Arbeit*, in which he develops a theology of earthly realities.

KARL RAHNER, S.J., internationally known theologian, is on the philosophical faculty of the University of Munich. At present he is editing the ten-volume *Lexicon für Theologie und Kirche* and the new pastoral encyclopedia *Sacramentum Mundi*, which will appear simultaneously in five languages. The most recently translated of Father Rahner's more than 700 books and articles include *Free Speech in the Church*, *Encounters with Silence*, *The Eternal Year*, and volumes III, IV and V of *Theological Investigations*.

JOHANNES B. METZ teaches fundamental theology at the University of Münster. He studied in Munich and Innsbruck, where he received his doctorate in theology under Karl Rahner. He is the co-editor of the periodical "Concilium" and the two-volume work *Gott in Welt*. His main writings have been on Christian anthropology and the problems of carrying out faith in practice.

HEINRICH SCHLIER is professor of New Testament Scripture at the University of Bonn. His writings on the epistles include *Christ and the Church in the Epistle to the Ephesians* and *The Epistle to the Galatians*. Since 1958 he has been serving with Karl Rahner as co-editor of *Quaestiones Disputatae*.

WALTER DÜRIG is professor of liturgy and pastoral theology at the University of Munich. He also serves as director of the Georgianum Seminary there. His book *Imago* is a study of the theology and terminology of the Roman liturgy. In his most recent work, he discusses the future of the liturgical renewal.

Leo Scheffczyk, a frequent contributor to German-language theological journals, teaches dogmatic theology at the University of Tübingen. In his books he has taken up the themes of a Christian secular piety and creation and divine Providence; his latest work compares the modern with the biblical image of man.

M.-D. Chenu, O.P., formerly a professor of religious history at the Sorbonne, was for fifteen years editor of *Revue des Sciences Philosophiques et Théologiques*. A *peritus* at the Second Vatican Council, he has written, among many works, *The Theology of the Twentieth Century*, *Theology as the Science of the Thirteenth Century*, and *Is Theology a Science?*

Heinz Robert Schlette, after studying philosophy and theology at Münster and Munich, became assistant professor at the University of Freiburg. Since 1962 he has been professor of philosophy at the Pedagogische Hochschule in Bonn. Among other themes, he has written on freedom, Soviet humanism, and the theology of religions. Two of his works have been published in *Quaestiones Disputatae*.

PART ONE

The Christian Looks at the World

The Changing Character of the Christian Understanding of the World

by ALFONS AUER

I. THE MEDIEVAL UNDERSTANDING OF THE WORLD

A. THE CONCEPT OF WORLD

THE MIDDLE AGES would not recognize our modern inquiry into the world as world, the world per se. We may no more expect a direct statement of this issue from the medieval mind than we may from the New Testament. The problem of the worldliness of the world can really come into perspective only when the "horizon of the world's nothingness with this horizon's origin and claims"[1] has been surmounted. On this point we must agree with H. R. Schlette.

But Schlette traces the absence of a theological treatment of this question in medieval theology to the fact that "the world as world, because of the ever-valid belief in creation, could not at all be categorized."[2] This is true only of the specifically medieval form and vitality of belief in creation, but not of the belief in creation as such. Otherwise, one would have to maintain that the man who believes in creation could not possibly comprehend the world as it is in itself. We would prefer, rather, to arrive at such an understanding in the scholastic spirit, which recognized that the self-subsistence of creatures and yet their total dependence on God were not mutually exclusive concepts.[3]

Since the Middle Ages did not reflect on the problem of the world in the modern sense of the term, it is hardly surprising that the concept of "world" was not clearly determined. In the theological and spiritual literature of this period, "world" means the God-created totality of visible and invisible realities—the creation of God, the goodness and beauty of which are so often enthusiastically praised.

In the spiritual literature, however, this doctrinal concept of the world is considerably overlapped by a one-sided emphasis on its evanescence and frailty, which have experienced an extreme intensification in the sinful disordering of the world. The text of 1 John 2:15–16, in which the world appears as the embodiment of evil, as a triad of possessions, pomp and inordinate desire, acquires an almost canonical status in the *De contemptu mundi* literature from Ambrose to Erasmus. Very often we come across a view of the world as life outside the cloister, life amidst the allurements and temptations of earthly goods.[4] In this stratification of the medieval understanding of the world, we can expect to find both positive and negative factors.

B. POSITIVE FACTORS IN THE MEDIEVAL UNDERSTANDING OF THE WORLD

The truths of revelation form an obvious foundation for the medieval understanding of the world: God, the supreme Lord, has created the world out of nothing and keeps it in existence through his creative presence. The disaster resulting from the sin of man was fundamentally overcome when God, through his Son, embraced the fallen world in grace. At the end of history, by the power of God, the world will be brought home into his glory. These truths of revelation no doubt were sometimes watered down in a spiritualistic sense; by and large they were not able to develop their full spiritual import. This situation is especially true of the early Christian centuries, when the Christian will to realization pursued a primarily introspective course.

The picture changed at the beginning of the Middle Ages, when a new dynamism poured into Christianity from the Germanic realm. The Christian learned to understand the world as a gift and assignment from God. He actively sensed his profession as a calling; this received its first recognizable form among the leading classes of society—the princes and knights—but at an early date began to appeal to all ranks, down to the merchants, horse dealers and innkeepers. This sense of profession was being cultivated in guilds and crafts long before Thomas Aquinas pondered over his theological teaching on vocation.

Christian mysticism saw in every creature the realization of a divine thought; it taught man to look for the traces of God in the world in order to find the creator. Medieval symbolism is likewise unthinkable without a candid respect for creatures, even though, on the other hand, it frightened man away far too quickly from their intrinsic value. Since the Renaissance and the Age of Humanism, not a few authors have praised the *dignitas hominis*. The theological motives had been at hand since patristic times: man's origin from God, his destiny to be an image of God and to rule in the world, his calling to communion with Christ and his final fulfilment in the glory of heaven.

This theological evaluation of man was, in principle at least, the common property of the entire Middle Ages. Man appeared as the center of the world, created in order that through him the world might be brought back to God. In general, however, God's image appeared founded not in the whole man, but rather in his spirituality and freedom. Also, the place of man in the world was explained not so much from his own make-up as from divine ordinance. Man's value lay in his function as God's trustee in the world.

In the twelfth century we hear the first faint suggestions of our modern problem regarding the worldliness of the world. An attempt was made to recognize the inherent value in the realms of earthly realities and to obtain a clearer view of the true relation between the orders of creation and salvation. Thomas Aquinas forcefully demonstrated that despite contingency and creative dependence there was still room for the genuine reality of the world as such. The French Dominican R. A. Gauthier asserts that it was to St. Thomas's credit that "he made possible the formation of a typically lay mentality" alongside the monastic spirituality directly aligned to God. This typically lay mentality was "made available for men who continue to have obligations toward the world which has returned to its worldliness [*profanité*]." [5]

We find in the Middle Ages only the beginnings of the kind of inquiry into the world pursued by modern science. But man's knowledge of the world and his understanding of the basic aspects of human existence were viewed together in the bold systems of medieval philosophy and theology. The great *Summas* not only uniformly recapitulated the total learning of the time, but above all offered an ultimate interpretation by integrating this learning with the statements of revelation as reflected upon in theology.[6]

C. NEGATIVE FACTORS IN THE MEDIEVAL UNDERSTANDING OF THE WORLD

The positive factors we have just considered never came to the fore historically as we might have expected. The basic attitude of the Middle Ages was one-sidedly that of flight from the world. The monastic, ascetical ideal prevailed also in the world; medieval Christianity was predominantly shaped by monks. Its ideal of life had a fascinating effect also upon laymen; one thought he could serve God best and most uncompromisingly when he bade farewell to the world. Numerous writings bear the title: *De contemptu mundi, De miseria conditionis humanae* and *Ars morendi*.[7]

Unquestionably the "divinistical mentality of the Fathers" (Y.

Congar) had lasting repercussions in the Middle Ages. One properly adhered to the dogmatic assertions, but in the area of Christian living many an escapist tendency of Stoic, Manichaean and Neo-Platonistic origin crept in. It was an easy matter to give such tendencies a biblical garb and thereby create the impression of a kind of super-Christianity. The Bible was held in great esteem; but its interpretation was attempted in a quite arbitrary manner. Qoheleth 1:2 [8] and 1 John 2:15–16 [9] were the most frequently quoted passages in the *De contemptu mundi* literature. These passages were interpreted to maintain simply that Sacred Scripture in its totality demanded a contempt for the world.

Undoubtedly the attitude of many authors toward the world was aggravated by a certain decadence of the time, a gloomy estimation of their own religious situation, severe catastrophes such as famine, plague, devastation and war, and a bitter personal fortune. Perhaps the strongest motive for adopting an attitude of contempt for the world, however, was the need for peace and security. Possessions, pomp and inordinate desire cause man a plethora of troubles; contempt for them would free him from many worldly hardships and burdens and would open to him a more reliable path to salvation.[10]

What H. R. Schlette states about Hugo of St. Victor holds for almost the entire output of medieval ascetical literature. According to the religious consciousness and experience of the time, goodness of creatures was overshadowed by the reality of man's fallen nature. This outlook "often awakened a harsh dualistic impression." [11] Beginning with its composition of matter and form, the world presented a danger which reached extreme acuteness in the disaster of sin; sinfulness appeared to be the ruling characteristic of the contemporary situation in salvation history. This conception of the world as materiality (corporeality, sexuality) and especially as the domain of evil clearly pushed into the background of religious consciousness the doctrinally held belief in the world as creation. Man must be protected from the fascination of the world. And the best way to do this was to concentrate on the darker side of the world, to screen one's eyes from the allurement of the world and to fix them squarely on God.

D. AN APPRAISAL OF THE MEDIEVAL UNDERSTANDING OF THE WORLD

In appraising the Middle Ages, we should not be content with the declaration that, thanks to the fidelity to dogmatic teachings, false principles were time and again clearly and resolutely averted. The far-reaching pedagogical and moral depreciation of the world opened the door, and kept it open for too long, to many a tendency stemming from pre- and non-Christian sources to disavow the world.[12]

Yet we should not assess the Middle Ages solely from the modern viewpoint. In contrast to the Middle Ages, modern times have certainly much more clearly seen the intrinsic nature of the world and the obligation inherent in it. The medieval understanding of the world appears to many to be primitive, barbaric and unenlightened. But we cannot consider history in this way. "The sole criterion by which an age can be rightly measured is the question: How far in it does the fullness of human existence expand to and attain a genuine meaningfulness? This occurred in the Middle Ages in a manner which associates it with the greatest periods of history." [13]

In the greatness of the Middle Ages, its very limitations become all the more apparent. No other age was able to achieve to the same degree a blending of the terrestrial and heavenly kingdoms into a single universal order in which the temporal realms were directly ordered to the spiritual reality of the Church, and even—in order to maintain this order—directly or at least indirectly subjugated to ecclesiastical regulation. This unitary order necessarily resulted in a situation in which temporal matters were not adequately considered with respect to their inherent value nor sufficiently seen as fashioned according to their own laws. In the long run, the sacred order of the Middle Ages amounted to the same thing as Monophysitism. This point will be dealt with later in this article.

II. THE MODERN PROFANE UNDERSTANDING OF THE WORLD

A. THE PHENOMENON OF MODERN PROFANENESS

"To the question of in what way those things that have being exist, the modern consciousness answers: as nature, as the subject of personality, and as culture. These three phenomena are interrelated; they mutually limit and perfect one another. Their framework signifies a final entity beyond which nothing can further be referred. It needs no foundation from anywhere else, nor does it tolerate a higher norm." [14]

The modern view of the world no longer sees nature as the creation of God, but rather as an autonomous universe standing on its own two feet and needing no other basis or standard from without. The modern man wrenches himself, as well as nature, from the authority of God and enthrones himself as the autonomous master of his own life. He is no longer the subordinate who receives the world as a fief from God and, against his own will, fashions it in obedience. The modern man sees only himself. Astonished, man discovers himself as an individual and suddenly becomes self-important.[15] He now represents only himself in civilization; he comes to envisage himself as creator, and thereby also frees his work in the world from obedience to God. This autonomy is the pith of modern secularism: world and man stand by themselves, having their value, law and goal in themselves; there are no references to the transcendent. The voice of the Church, which strives toward an understanding of the world and life from revelation, is rejected as that of a foreign intruder (heteronomy).

The increasingly conscious "autonomous reason" of his own power further induces man gradually to understand and shape all earthly spheres according to an immanent set of laws. The sheer rules of the game prevail: power determines politics; mere profit, economics; pure form, art; possible disposability, technology. The Middle Ages had bound up all these spheres into its whole temporal-spiritual order, whose purpose and end it believed to be found in revelation. The way to freedom and salvation proceeded through the acknowledgment of these factors. In modern secularism there is a "self-liberation through knowledge." [16]

Reason finds the objective laws of order; reason verifies its ethical obligation; reason sees the individual orders in an over-all interpretation of man and world together. The statements and claims of a self-revealing God wishing to speak to man no longer have any place here. One concedes to earlier generations that they had to resort to such notions. But one is sure that it was a question only of a veiled kind of human self-assertion: man simply projected outwardly his own longings and needs. There was no basis at all in reality for these concepts, and it was therefore incumbent upon an enlightened age finally to break through to the truth.

Profaneness or secularism thus means a general intellectual attitude in which reality is accounted for from a purely inner-worldly mode of thinking. The truths of revelation and their interpretation by churches and theologians remain not only *de facto*, but also consciously and intentionally excluded from consideration, because the truth ascertained by reason alone is denied them. Religion can still be allowed a private and interior place of its own, so long as no objections against state, society, technology, art, or science ensue from it. In the pure, absolute profaneness, every outlet to the transcendent is excluded.

By the terms "secularizing" or "making worldly," we understand the historical process which led to the mentality of profaneness or secularism. This historical process is judged within the profaneness itself as a liberation, the coming of man to himself. From the standpoint of religion, it is characterized as the culpable, or in any case fatal, breaking-away from the coordination of the mundane orders with religion as its center, a coordination prescribed and expressed by the order of creation and salvation.[17]

B. THE CRISIS OF MODERN PROFANENESS

In his book *The End of the Modern World,* R. Guardini offers not only a phenomenological view of modern profaneness, but also points to the elements which have led to its crisis.[18] For several decades now man's relationship to nature has been in transition. Nature is no longer the kind, all-protecting "Mother Nature"; rather it is the medium within which man's work is set out. In technology man experiences the dimensions of this potentiality, but also the converging dangers. The more he scientifically investigates and technically masters nature, the more unfamiliar and hostile it appears to him.

The autonomous individual, who a short time ago so emphatically extolled personality as the "greatest boon of mortal men," suddenly finds himself constrained by the very forces of those structures which a perfected technology has developed in all areas of life and which now relentlessly regulate his freedom and his whole way of living. Man comes to learn that the more he organizes all spheres of life, the more he is treated as an object, a functionary. He no longer sees himself on the lonely summit of a unique and creative self-experience; rather, in the phenomenon of the masses, he feels himself restricted by the structures around him, which penetrate to his innermost being. He is afraid of what appears to him to be the heart of his human existence.

A final peril for him arises from the very civilization he created: his hope for a never-ending progress, a life of prosperity, freedom and peace is dampened. He sees the development of undreamed-of potentialities as an accomplished fact, but a profound skepticism overcomes him as to whether every growth in technical might is really an enrichment of his person and of his solidarity with the community.

Because he is not used to the power so quickly devolved upon him, he loses his feeling of security in his control over technology. His ever-prodigious technical works seem to have detached themselves from him and set themselves up as an independent power opposed to him. Much to his dismay he discovers that the chaos of nature, which he had harnessed and against which he had safeguarded himself, might with its sinister force overtake him, and that the final situation might become much worse than the first.

Modern profaneness finds itself in its ultimate intensification. In contrast, its earlier forms—the autonomy of the state, of science, of art, and so forth—appear as harmless child's play. Natural science and technology in the last one hundred years have invested pristine worldliness with an importance which it did not have (at least not recognizably for most people) so long as it concerned itself with reality in a purely speculative or artistic manner. Technocratic profaneness with the full impetus of its economic, technical, social and political structures has taken the wind out of the sails of the human person. The inquiry into the meaning of the world and of human existence is thereby silenced. "Vitalism and existentialism express the self-understanding of this secularism. They base themselves insistently on the grounds of a pure vitality and existential receptivity that precede and are outside reason; they then converge in mystical solipsism." [19]

C. AN APPRAISAL OF MODERN PROFANENESS

It was stated that modern profaneness has reached a crisis, but this does not necessarily mean it has foundered, for every genuine crisis has within itself the possibility of a good denouement. Later it will become more evident how far this is true of modern profaneness. Here is not the place for any premature assertions as to whether the crisis of modern profaneness can be mastered either in a *pure* inner-worldly, or *only* in a Christian sense. In any case, the mere fact that modern profaneness has reached a crisis still does not absolve Christianity from its historical complicity in the secularization of the modern world; nor does it at all mean an approval of the present state of secularism.

We might be able to throw light on the whole situation by posing the concise question: What is the evaluation of modern profaneness from a theological viewpoint? From outright rejection, that is, the relentless indictment of modern profaneness because of the world's disavowal of God's acceptance of it in Christ, the appraisal passes to the express welcome of this evolution by those who see therein the new possibilities for the realization of Christianity. Before we turn to some opinions from Catholic and Protestant Evangelical theology, we should first briefly describe the religious-psychological approach to the problem. (We pass over a purely negative appraisal of this modern development, especially since it is nowadays scarcely treated in theological writings.)

1. A religious-psychological appraisal

C. H. Ratschow,[20] following P. Radin, holds that profaneness or, as he calls it, secularism, is a latent pitfall for every religion. His argument runs something like this: There are men everywhere who have no religious convictions or experiences; they tend to be a thoughtful, rational type of people. Because religion as the center of man's existence remains foreign to them, in their search for the meaning of existence they are compelled, so to speak, to set out in a purely worldly, secular and immanent manner and thus to depend upon their power of reason alone. These skeptics are a constant hidden danger to all religions.

But as the occasion presents itself, their rationalistic interpretation of world and life gains a considerable foothold and then in violent eruptions of "enlightenment" becomes historically actual, as in the case of Averroism and Nominalism during the Middle

Ages, the Renaissance and Humanism at the beginning of modern times and most visibly—picking up increasingly more momentum—since the Enlightenment of the seventeenth and eighteenth centuries.[21] This way of thinking undoubtedly plays an important part in the appreciation of modern profaneness.

Man, with his deep-rooted and lively experience of the absolute, always has the inclination to depreciate and reject what is finite and temporal precisely because it is not absolute. The absolute becomes the only thing; any truth the finite realities may have is thereby lost. One could say it is the function of profane thought to counteract such a neglect of the world and in that way also to help discover the full truth about God.

2. *An appraisal from Catholic theology*

With all due respect for the Middle Ages, Catholic theology has not let the positive elements of modern profaneness go unnoticed. We know that in the Middle Ages the absolute was often so one-sidedly emphasized that earthly realities could not fully unfold their genuine meaning. The modern age, on the contrary, has shoved the absolute *so far* into the background, even completely denying it, that the creatureliness of the world has been more and more obscured and sometimes totally impugned. Nevertheless, the created universe with its own existence and its own dignity stands out more clearly. The world has been seen as a reality, and explored and molded with great candor and objectivity. Modern man takes the world more seriously than his medieval counterpart could. R. Guardini characterizes this development in the modern relationship of man to the world as a "coming of age." [22]

According to J. B. Metz, modern profaneness originated not in opposition to, but on account of Christianity. It is initially a Christian event brought on by Christian impulses. The pantheism of the ancients never allowed the world to become entirely worldly, because it never let God become entirely divine. It was lacking the notion of a transcendent creator; the divine seemed to be an element of the world. A Christianity which rightly understands itself must appear "not as increasing divinization but precisely as a mounting removal of divinity from the world, and in this sense as a profanation of the world." [23] To the pagans of old, the Christians were the real "atheists."

If only Christianity had taken more seriously its belief in creation with all the ensuing consequences, it would not then have fallen so deeply into theological and religious embarrassment as a result of the modern secularization of the world. Certainly the Christian believed that God created the world and constantly kept it in existence. But the believer did not see clearly enough that precisely through the mysteries of creation and Christ, through the creation and adoption of the world in grace, there occurred "the original and radical liberation of the world to its own character and properties, to the undisguised reality of its non-divinity." [24] It is one of the tragic events in the history of Christianity that the secularization of the world, to which it gave the impetus, *de facto* has prevailed contrary to Christianity's concrete historical understanding of the world. And not least of all because of the opposition of Christians, this secularization of the world has taken on such militantly secular features.

Modern profaneness, however, implies a protest not only against the pantheistic undoing of the world as it is in itself (through a merging with God), but also against its Monophysitic undoing, which happened in the Middle Ages through the merging of the world with the church. A conscious intention to respect and safeguard the world and the church as they are in themselves should in no way, at least not generally, be imputed to the supporters of the secular movement. But in their protest against the expropriation of the world by the church, they have brought to bear the right of the world, and its true nature, in the face of illegitimate ecclesiastical claims. And right here there is something of theological significance. Not only is there the charism of *agape*, through which the world is brought home to Christ, there is also the charism of *eros*, which recognizes and loves the truth and beauty of the world. How could something not recognized and loved be brought home to Christ?

Certainly men on the road to modern profaneness are at fault for having spurned God, their Creator and Saviour. But no one can say whether there are many or few who proceed against the clear dictate of their conscience. On the other hand, the one-sided exaggeration of the absoluteness of God and the more or less Monophysitic interpretation of the relationship of church and world have in no small way contributed to the fact that the self-subsistence of the world has been so overshadowed. Since man is seldom a master of moderation, it is not surprising that the reaction to such developments took the radical form of an autonomous profaneness.[25] Modern profaneness has in fact helped—and perhaps even given the decisive impulses—to rectify the one-sided constructions of the Christian understanding of the world. Modern profaneness has also suggested to Christianity new and legitimate factors in man's relationship to the world that can be integrated into the actuality of salvation.

3. *An appraisal from Evangelical Protestant theology*

We can sketch just a few opinions—and these only very hastily—from Evangelical Protestant theology, which comes to terms in a frank and penetrating way with the phenomenon of modern profaneness.[26]

D. Bonhoeffer has expounded the relationship between Christian faith and the modern lack of religion. On the one hand, the church is to blame for the modern process of secularization; on the other, this process of secularization is only possible within a Christian background and should for that reason be assessed as "a historical execution of what is already founded in the Christian faith itself in its relation to the world: namely, the removal of divinity from the world."[27]

On the whole, D. Bonhoeffer has no regrets, therefore, about the rise of a "world coming of age," of a world without religion. Along with K. Barth, he supports the conviction that there should never even be an attempt to make room once again for religion in the secularized world. The coming generation will be one completely without religion.[28] Yet here lies a new and great opportunity for the Christian message. For this message—in a world without religion— must also be without religion. Today and in the future, religion may be demanded as a prerequisite or way to faith just as unessentially as the Jewish circumcision was earlier. The world's lack of religion testifies to God's powerlessness in the world. And in this situation salvation is found, as became manifest in the crucifixion. "For I determined not to know anything among you, except Jesus Christ and him crucified" (1 Cor. 2:2).[29]

D. Bonhoeffer's summons for a "non-religious interpretation of biblical concepts" plays a central role in the Evangelical Protestant discussion about the problem of secularism. Religion is here classified with the "law." K. Barth has also seen in the Christian faith the fundamental antithesis to religion, and with good reason, if one regards religion as the attempt to have God and his work of redemption at one's own disposal and through the act of religion alone to force one's way to God. The "religious interpretation" of biblical concepts is then simply "legal interpretation." Understood in this way, "religious interpretation" in the end excludes what D. Bonhoeffer means by "non-religious interpretation."

This "non-religious interpretation" involves three things: first, a Christological interpretation, that is, in theological thought Jesus Christ is at stake: What does Christ really mean for us today?; second, a concrete interpretation, that is, intellectual sincerity must also be respected in theology, and the question strictly posed: What do we really believe?; third, an interpretation of the faith, that is, the theological thought must be adjusted to the message and must answer the question: How can Christ become the salvation also of those without religion?[30]

W. Hartmann sees in the "breakdown of profaneness and of the autocracy of the human capability to do everything" the only possibility for a new link with the autonomous man. The proper stewardship of the world as God's inheritance can hardly be the affair of an autonomous reason, because this reason consciously disengages itself from administering the world in the spirit of the creator and lawgiver. Any action in the world may not be separated from faith; solicitude for the world must not pass over to the autonomous reason alone. For when man rejects the gospel, he inevitably falls—in some way or other—"under the law." He further runs aground every time he tries by his own efforts to account for himself and the world. Human existence cannot be produced, but rather is acquired only from God. The modern profane man must therefore be allowed to guide his existence "under the law."

At the same time, however, W. Hartmann warns that any attempt to exploit the failure of secularism for religious purposes—in order to overcome its crisis—leads to an "obsolete religious outlook toward the world." Secularism cannot be rescinded; it must be surmounted by looking ahead. This looking-ahead also lies in the "non-religious interpretation" of the Christian content of faith.[31]

As with D. Bonhoeffer and W. Hartmann, so also for F. Gogarten the coming-of-age of mankind appears as the fruit of the Christian faith. The one under age is the man "under the law." Through belief in the gospel, man reaches majority: he is admitted to "sonship." Through faith he becomes a "co-heir of Christ" (Rom. 8:17), and in his alliance with Christ he bears a responsibility for the world. The Christian, who in sonship is set free for responsible action in the world, must by all means "hold back" his faith. Should faith itself attend to the doings of the world, it would wrong both itself and the world. Indeed, faith—and only faith—knows all about the world. But the believer must restrain this knowledge; it is not for him to desire to take the entirety of the world upon himself, because he would then fall under its law.[32]

Similarly, H. Schreiner affirms the genuine reality of the world, its self-subsistence, and its freedom from all external pressure and —what he especially stresses—from demoniac secularism, which leads necessarily to totalitarianism. Yet for him faith in no way remains "held back"; it is rather the only guarantee of a genuine world-formation. It must operate very concretely in the different domains. On this point H. Schreiner differs from F. Gogarten. This variance becomes even more evident when H. Schreiner to some extent offers concrete suggestions for the self-subsistence of all worldly realities found in the conscience bound up in God.[33]

Finally, H. Kraemer asserts that the initial excitement of the awakening has long since died down. Through the scientific and technical control of the powers of nature, modern autonomy has fallen into a "Babylonian pandemonium," the like of which history has rarely experienced. The coming-of-age of reason faces a multitude of modern idolatries. The progress of science has led not only to a heightened self-confidence, but also to a menacing spiritual dissipation and a sometimes insufferable loss of norms. The modern profane man has been outplayed by his own conquests and is no longer able to remain their master.

In the course of this evolution in modern profaneness, a number of areas have been snatched away from the church (education, social welfare, and so forth), so that the church has had to submit to a far-reaching privation of functions. But the work of the church has thereby become especially problematic in that a fundamental religious understanding of the world and life can "no longer find a place" in the fundamentally secularized orientation. And yet modern profaneness also has a positive meaning for the church: the relative autonomy of worldly spheres has become more clearly evident, and the church sees herself unavoidably compelled to rethink her own understanding of herself and the world.[34]

III. A THEOLOGY OF EARTHLY REALITIES

The task of theology is to abstract the truths of revelation from the sources, to thoughtfully enter into them, to order them into a complete picture, and to impart them to contemporary society. The truth theology has to proclaim is the one assigned to it; it is a truth which is to be found time and again and which should be expressed in an up-to-date manner. The way of theology proceeds from above, from God to the world and to man. Its method is a deductive one.

The following treatise, although it begins with reflections on the self-subsistence of the world, is only seemingly inductive. Even a "theology of earthly realities" is bound to the deductive method. But the theological answer should be given whence the question arises: it should seek the modern profane man where he exists. This speculative treatment will not, therefore, take up the problem of the self-subsistence of the world in order to keep the reflection strictly to its object, for this could be accomplished in other ways. This procedure is presented rather only as a help to make it clear to the reader—especially to one not versed in theology—that the theological consideration and statement do keep to the point.[35]

A. THE SELF-SUBSISTENCE OF EARTHLY REALITIES

What does this thesis concerning the independence of earthly realities mean? How is it to be explained?

1. The concept of the thesis

By the "worldly domain" we understand the different forms of human association and the material order as well as the activity connected with them: work, profession, society, science, culture, art, technology, and economy. These worldly domains all have a bona fide existence of their own. They have their own proper and valid existence, and thereby also their own proper meaning and system of laws to which man in his knowledge and action must submit. Their proper existence must remain intact even when the philosopher or believer sees in them a transcendental relationship. Philosophy preserves an existence of its own as opposed to theology, as does culture as opposed to piety and mysticism, and economics as opposed to charity. There is not only God, but also the world. There is not only religion, but also economics, technology, art and science. And they all have an existence of their own. Religion cannot simply be everything; it cannot of itself dictate an order and posit norms for other fields. These areas must have "their own laws and their own, at least relative, autonomy in order really to subsist at all." [36]

He who believes that the world has come into existence through the Word cannot find it difficult to perceive that order, law-abidingness and meaningfulness prevail in the world as a whole and in all the component parts of the world. The more God puts the world, which is dependent upon him, on its own two feet, all the more he supports it in its own being; so the more divine his work appears. In the teaching of the natural law, the fact that earthly realms have their own set of laws is expressly recognized. Man must yield to the natural order, to the objective logic inherent in the individual worldly domains, and thereby uncover that truth and call forth that order which lies in the things themselves.

Since the beginning of modern times, science has devoted itself with growing interest to earthly realities as such. The result is that understanding of the world and of human life has been deepened and broadened to a remarkable degree. Man has become another person; he behaves differently toward the world and toward himself. His increased insight into the orders and laws of the world in great and small things vividly brings home to him the meaning of an existence that is both self-subsistent and endowed with its own laws. Science, in laying bare the truth of the world, has made a contribution which, however, should not be overestimated.

The insight that the world is temporally and spatially limited, and therefore measurable, also belongs to the perceptions of natural science. According to the ancients, the cosmos stood autonomous in itself. Beyond the cosmos, nothing further could be imagined. The cosmos itself was its own basis, law and meaning; the divine and the human were enclosed in it. The limited and measurable cosmos of modern natural science, however, cannot be understood as something absolute.[37]

More and more the conviction prevails that by measurability alone we cannot arrive at a decisive quality of the real. Even the smallest things refer to something beyond themselves: "Through themselves they point beyond themselves to the most profound depths." They point to man, in whom alone they become conscious and expressable.[38]

It goes without saying that theology neither could nor would want to shy away from the findings of modern science; rather, science can provide theology with some very fruitful impulses. The belief in the constancy of knowledge and of culture is theologically outdated. Even Thomas Aquinas thought that every good thing had essentially been discovered by the dawn of the new era, about the time of St. Paul, and that all further discoveries could only be inferior ones. As God rested on the seventh day, so man also, after the birth of Christ, rested from all the work of civilization and restricted himself to the preservation of what had been achieved.

Thomas certainly knew that there would be new findings and cultural advances in the future course of history. But since the coming of Christ, they could not be good of themselves, but only insofar as they served religious purposes. In contrast to this view, Pius XII clearly stated: "Every human cognition, even when not of a religious character, has in itself its own value and sovereignty; it is, however, a participation in God's infinite knowledge. When it is used to elucidate God and questions concerning the divine, it thereby receives a new, higher value and consecration." [39]

2. *The meaning of the thesis*

We have already shown how the modern secularistic evolution has carried the self-subsistence of the world too far in an *autonomous* direction. Only the one-sidedly rational has been acknowledged; any foundation of this self-subsistence in a transcendental relationship has been denied. The claim of a divine revelation has appeared as a heteronomous presumption. Since the Renaissance and Humanism, but above all since the Enlightenment of the seventeenth and eighteenth centuries, the consequences of this secularistic conception have been more rigorously thought out and steadily realized. Gradually the worldly arenas have shaken themselves loose from that guardianship of the church which was so matter-of-fact to the medieval man. The lords with their politics were the first to break away; then followed the common welfare and city life, scientific thought and morality, and finally the conscience of the people and their daily experience of pleasure and pain.

We have also shown how this development was a reaction—one necessarily expected, so to speak, from a historical-theological point of view—to the *integralistic* appropriation of the self-subsistence of the world. Here we should recall two forms of this appropriation, and what we have learned from their effects.

First, the world as world must not be plunged into the absoluteness of God. The fact that there is a higher being is no tacit permission to efface, as it were, a lower one. The absoluteness of God must be interpreted not in itself, in the abstract, but rather from the concrete history of salvation set in motion and sustained by God. The absoluteness of God must be interpreted in such a way that it brooks the "pluralism" of things. In the Catholic teaching of the *analogia entis* (analogy of being), the absoluteness of God is doctrinally expressed plainly enough, but its concrete understanding and realization in faith have often been *de facto* disregarded. This understanding and realization in faith were more orientated to Greek than to biblical thinking. Otherwise it would have been seen that God's creative love, in its giving and its being-content to leave a being as it is, carries with it the possibility and also the guarantee for the world as it is in itself.

As to the second form of appropriation, the understanding of the world per se must never again be Monophysitically atomized in the church. The duality of orders, rightly understood, must remain untouched for the entire duration of salvation history. The concern of the church, and of those in the church who dedicate themselves to theology and kerygma, is focused on the integration of the world into the history of salvation. With such a viewpoint, it can easily happen that the "one thing necessary" in tow, as it were, becomes the only thing. In relation to this one thing, everything else becomes unimportant; to acknowledge that the other has its own reality even seems sacrilegious and sinfully secularistic. Those who know their history well and who interpret it have declared often enough how strongly and persistently this misunderstanding—call it divinism, hierocracy, or ecclesiological monism—has stamped concrete Christianity.

Just as autonomism has misconstrued the transcendental grounding of the world, so divinism has failed to appreciate that the world has a reality of its own. In order to do justice to historical truth, we should show, however, that theology has actually always been on the way to a denouement in which the world's deeper dimension and value are preserved.

In Christian antiquity (Justin, Clement of Alexandria), the *logos spermatikos* was everywhere operative and therefore could resolutely support the right of culture within the church. Toward the end of the fifth century, Pope Gelasius I made a sharp distinction between the spiritual and worldly realms of power, tracing both directly to Christ. This concept came to the fore time and again from the Middle Ages down to Leo XIII, who expressly made it his own. Beginning in the twelfth century (Suger, Abelard, Godfrey of St. Victor), theology began to reflect more keenly upon the self-subsistence of the earthly spheres. This was the time of the discovery of the world's reality as such. In the Thomistic concept of creation, the self-subsistence of creatures is definitively anchored in theology. Leo XIII concretized this view in numerous statements which recognized the "necessary autonomy" of the worldly orders and "an area of justifiable and legitimate freedoms." [40]

In *Quadragesimo anno,* Pius XI cites Leo's remark that the Church believes it would be wrong for her to interfere without just cause in earthly concerns. He rejects the authority of the Church to make assertions upon technical matters, since she has neither the means nor the competence for this. The competence of the Church confines itself to "what has a relation to the moral law." [41]

Catholic social science sees here the unequivocal recognition that the various areas of civilization are self-subsistent and possess their own inherent system of laws. When the Pope says that economics has its own "principles," [42] he means exactly what we wish to express with the still relatively new ideas of self-subsistence (*Eigenständigkeit*) and "necessary" autonomy (*Eigengesetzlichkeit*): namely, that economics and all other fields have their own basis of being upon which they rest, and their own laws which flow from this basis of being and are therefore indispensable. O. v. Nell-Breuning sees in the phrase *"suis utuntur principiis"* ("things operate by their own principles") "a classical formulation of our own terms of self-subsistence and 'necessary' autonomy." [43]

In the evolving "theology of earthly realities," the earthly spheres —the human and the material—prevail as a proper theme in theology itself, thus no longer being relegated only to sociocultural philosophy and ethics. This "theology of earthly realities," in which the world as world finally is treated theologically, will have to consider more exactly the relationship of the emancipation of the worldly orders to their own self-subsistence, and, in doing so, must overcome many an integralistic prejudice.

B. THE RELATIVE SELF-SUBSISTENCE OF EARTHLY REALITIES

As we already stated, the assertion that the earthly realities are self-subsistent and have laws which are proper to themselves does not express the full truth. This assertion must be integrated further so that the foundation of the worldly orders in a transcendental relationship of being can also be seen and recognized in reference not only to God the Creator but also to Christ the Head. These integrating statements about the world can be made only by theology, for their content has become accessible only through revelation. In the history of salvation, the transcendental determination of the world is thus presented in two great stages: in the mystery of creation and in the mystery of Christ. The latter develops itself in the Church throughout history, and only with the second coming of Christ will come to a full revelation and realization.

The first level of the relative self-subsistence
of earthly realities is their creatureliness,
that is, their relationship to God the Creator

This statement must be set forth in its essential content.

a) *The world is created by God:* In an act of radical freedom and love, the world is placed in being out of nothing; by the same divine freedom and love it is continually preserved in existence. This creative action of God is accomplished through the Word, and for that reason certain *rationes seminales,* certain values and laws of order, are grounded in the world. Whatever possibilities and realities the world comprises come therefore from God.

This is the first decisive integration to which modern profaneness in its secularistic bent must yield. The world cannot be closed in on itself. The world need not necessarily exist; it does not therefore exist of itself, nor can it suffice of itself alone. The doctrine of creation draws the world into an immediate nearness to God and causes it to emerge as a direct and constantly actual expression of his creative love. The creator releases the world to a reality of its own, and so much so that the world appears to stand completely in itself; it is able to arouse the illusion of being fully autonomous.

b) Within the created universe the creator has set up an *ordering principle* comprising all things: *man*. Because it is ordered and meaningful, the world is present wholly in each of its components and is to be encountered in any—even the smallest—part. In man, however, the world is pre-eminently represented. The world is created for man and can find completion only through him. He is able to apprehend the world and thereby give things their names. He is entrusted by the creator with the task of fulfilling the world by his dominion in it. The world is the place of his existence, his "extended corporeality" (J. M. Scheeben). Since man is its center and head, this cosmos—in varying degrees—personally resounds with human corporeality into its uttermost ramifications apparently remote from man.

Sacred Scripture has not reflectively concerned itself with this anthropocentrism of the cosmos. K. Rahner notes that the anthropological truths of the Bible to a large extent employ categories drawn solely from an objective world, as well as ontology obtainable from these categories, "so that there is a danger of missing the theological individuality of man and seeing him, in a sheer objective approach, as a piece of the world." But the scriptural truths nevertheless have a clearly discernible "anthropological apex" insofar as they envision man as a spiritual, free person taken into partnership with God.[44] The fact that man is the image of God does not allow any evaluation of him as a stage in the development of the cosmos, as a being bound up in the same way as all the other beings, whereby he receives an even lower position than many others.[45]

J. B. Metz has recently shown that in Thomas Aquinas there is a speculative break-through from the ancient Greek cosmocentrism in which man is practically lost in the universe—or at any rate receives no special place in it—to the biblical-Christian anthropocentrism. The cosmos is now situated in the horizon of man, rather than man in the horizon of the cosmos. Man is no longer arranged as an arbitrary part in the universe. "The being of those things that exist is rather viewed and determined from this human subjectivity." In man, being, taken altogether, is very decidedly present. Subjectivity thus becomes "the primary place for the accessibility of being; thought is seen as making-present of being." In man, then, the universe is for the first time really present to itself.[46]

In this spirit of St. Thomas, J. Hommes speaks of a "human conditioning" or "personal meaning" of nature. Nature is fully immersed in the life of man; it is the "instrument of his existence," the "concrete part of his essence." Nature, with its personal conditioning, is given to man, but it demands at the same time man's own "independent spiritual-personal activity," which he can fruitfully unfold only in cooperation with other men in directing nature. "The human-personal conditioning of nature is something given to man in his existence, and therefore, as such, taken over by him as a determination of his very self. Man's ability to handle nature—as the tool of his existence—and his ability to handle the rational—as a possible way home—find themselves united in the human handling of the processes of nature."[47]

Christian anthropocentrism is obviously not only compatible with theocentrism but even grounded in it, for man has been placed by God the Creator in the center of the world. This Christian anthropocentrism is pregnant with meaning for an understanding of the world from the standpoint of salvation history.

History is only possible to the extent that a person is involved. The only history is that of man.

Because the cosmos, as the "extended corporeality of man," is personally conditioned, human history must also become cosmic history. This means first of all that the destiny of the cosmos can be understood only as a consequence adherent to human-personal history. The history of man precedes the fate of the universe as a causative factor and guides it onward. And secondly, history, shaped as it is out of the freedom of man, becomes necessary for the destiny of the cosmos. In the beginning, the unity of man and cosmos was a unity of glory. Through the sin of man it became an association in disaster. In the Second Adam and in man whom he has liberated, this unity is brought back into salvation and raised up even beyond the glory of the beginning. At the end of history, this unity of man and cosmos will enter into the glory of completion.

The ordering of the world's being to mankind also includes the potentiality that the world could become entangled in possible ruin as a result of the fault of man. This potentiality has become a historical reality. *Sin*, to be sure, has its origin in the freedom of the human person. Because the human personality is essentially socially and cosmically determined, the guilt stemming from the person must necessarily affect the social and cosmic realms. In Romans 8:20 f., Paul characterizes this consequence as *mataiotes* and *phthora*, as a true deterioration which became powerful in the world—and in things—after the curse of God and to which humanity is now subjugated as to a hard servitude.

One may interpret the "vanity" and "corruption" of Romans 8 as a partial loss of the transparency of creatures (an upsetting of values and laws of order), as the world's obstinacy toward man's will to form and rule, as its satanic misuse. In any event, time and again man comes to experience this corruption and is able to confirm this biblical truth from his own experience. The evangelist John describes the world as a sinister prodigy of power in which the evil spiritual potencies at work seduce man the pilgrim to a disordered use of the things of the world by the "lust of the flesh, and the lust of the eyes, and the pride of life" (1 John 2:15; cf. also John 12:31; 14:30; 16:11).

The Pauline and Johannine idea of the world as the epitome of evil does not cancel out the usual notion of the world—verified throughout the New Testament—as the embodiment of God's creation. The Pauline and Johannine idea intends rather to make more precise—to interpret—the latter truth within the framework of the history of salvation by bringing into account the mystery of sin with all its devastating consequences. The balanced interpretation of both aspects of the cosmos conception in the New Testament guards on the one hand against a naïve optimism which critically fails to appreciate the reality of evil and, on the other, against an unenlightened and basically unchristian pessimism which appears to exhaust all its energy of belief in the mystery of sin and has nothing left for the mysteries of creation and salvation.

c) Remaining to be established is the fact that from the very beginning, through God's creative will for the world, the world has been *finalized in Christ*. The incarnation of the eternal Word is the actual great goal of God's plan for the world. From the beginning, therefore, God not only implanted in his world all the "natural" forces and laws and values in such a way that they would expand themselves by virtue of an evolutional dynamism inherent in them and in the human spirit, but also embedded into his work of creation an altogether different dynamism, namely, the determination to salvation.

This statement includes the assertion that Christ would have become man even if there had been no sin. This so-called Scotistic viewpoint cannot be corroborated with absolute certitude; however, it is also not excluded by the New Testament. Were it to refer, as is sometimes said, to a merely possible or conceivable order, it would then surely be nothing more than a theological game. The question of whether Christ would have become incarnate even in the event there had been no sin is a question which the actual real order, the true plan of salvation, must help to resolve. The concrete fact of the development of salvation history, with its great stress on the concrete message of the New Testament, does not absolve us from the obligation of getting at the heart of the matter and exploring revelation for the "eternal" plan of salvation.

In any case, the plan of salvation culminates in the fact that the world created by God should be embraced in man and with man, its center, in Jesus Christ, and should be drawn into the inner life of God. The existence of the world and man has its foundation in Christ. We can never understand creation if we disregard him for whom it is determined, and this is revealed only in Jesus Christ.[48]

The second level of the relative self-subsistence of earthly realities is their relationship to Christ the Head

God plainly willed that his creation remain not just his "work," forever simply standing apart from him. He wanted to take his creation into his innermost being. "And this his good pleasure he purposed in him to be dispensed in the fullness of the times: to reestablish all things in Christ, both those in the heavens and those on the earth. In him, I say, in whom we also have been called by a special choice, having been predestined in the purpose of him who works all things according to the counsel of his will, to contribute to the praise of his glory—we who before hoped in Christ" (Eph. 1:9–12). What does St. Paul mean here?

a) The God-man is the head of mankind. Mankind is joined to this head as a body. The Fathers of the Church constantly emphasize this thought: Christ bears all men in himself; mankind as a whole is present in him. The human nature of Jesus Christ is, so to speak, a fulcrum which the eternal Word establishes in the world in order to draw all things to himself. Because his human nature stands in a real association with all human nature, Christ takes it into the solidarity of his person and thereby becomes the head of the human race. Now that mankind has become his body, he is able to elevate it to his communion with the Father, and also to let his own union with the Father overflow into this his body.

b) Henceforth man is the head and center of the cosmos. He is the living clasp by which the world of the spiritual and corporeal are fitted into one. In him the world encounters itself; in him it is present; in man it is seized into one. The world is primarily created for man so as to render possible to man his incarnate existence. As the "extended corporeality of man," the world is personally conditioned. It must therefore follow that the God-man, in becoming the head of the human race, also becomes the *head of the whole material creature*.

The material nature is indissolubly united to man, even as his own body is united to him, though to a lesser degree and contiguity. If man himself in his full body-soul existence is taken into communion with Christ, the remainder of creation cannot be left out. In this way the God-man, through his union with human nature, becomes conjointly the hypostasis of the entire creation: he bears this creation in himself as in a root. Everything man comprises in himself enters into his incorporation into the eternal Word. The Word made flesh becomes thus the new and actual place of the world.

c) But this is not to be understood to mean that a rigid and definitive state is produced, which would exclude any dynamism and further development. On the contrary, the eternal Word has united himself truly not with abstract essences, but rather with concrete men and things. Yet everything concrete stands in the stream of the historical. One can then say that the eternal Word has entered into full *solidarity with the total history* of man and his world. The God-man is not merely the encompassment into one of what is human and material, but also the encompassment of the development of man and things.

In himself, Christ sums up everything that is in history and carries it through into the last phase of the history of salvation. When this phase comes to an end, he will draw everything that is united to him into his return home into eternity. Among all men and things which are in the world and have their history in the world, there is nothing which could remain outside this union with Christ. There is not one thing that exists which does not have the vocation to be the "body of the Lord" and through him—in whatever form this may take—to participate in glory.

Jesus Christ bears the whole world and its history in his body. He is the one who gathers and summarizes into one, the universal mediator in whom the entire universe is "at home." In him the universe is where it belongs; in him it is brought to that place which was appointed to it ever since the beginning. The cosmos remains what it is, but it is inserted into the scope of its fulfilment. A definitive and irrevocable character marks this event which proceeds in Jesus Christ, beginning with the incarnation and provisionally realized with the ascension of our Lord into heaven. There is no relapse from Christ, nor is there anything in the inner history of the world which can surpass him.

"Man does not pass beyond Christ; in him the end of things is attained. He alone is the ultimate, the eternal youth of the world. He is always the new: Christ, beyond whom there is simply nothing else, in whom the end of things is reached. With him, humanity has entered into the essential event; henceforth we can expect no progress—no matter how great it may be—which will be of the same importance as what we already possess in Christ." [49]

Through this vision of history, Christianity is radically removed from that theory of evolution for which Christ is at most only one stage, however important, of transition. History proceeds further, century upon century, until the Lord's second coming. But what will be effected by his second coming has in the God-man already been made present on earth and abides forever. For this reason, everything that the world is presses essentially toward Christ, because it can find its integration in him alone. No person or thing can eliminate from the world this existential inclination.

The relationship to Christ the head is the second level of the relativity in which every self-subsistence of the earthly realities is grounded.

In Jesus Christ the world is definitively embraced by God. This is a fact of salvation history. The explanation of this fact (also of the form in which it is presented above) certainly needs more careful theological clarification in many respects.[50] The term *anakephalaiosis* from Ephesians 1:10 means that Christ has made the powers subject, that he has restored the original unity, and through the recapitulation to one dominion has brought the world home again to God. But may this and similar passages be interpreted in such a way that one speaks of the world as the "body of the Lord," when, however, by "body of the Lord" the Church is usually signified? Or would it be more accurate to say: Christ is indeed united with the cosmos, but nevertheless the body of Christ must be distinguished from what is only related to him?

At any rate, there are theologians who think that the cosmos and animal life are "manifestly" no part of the Mystical Body or of the whole Christ.[51] One must be very careful not to exaggerate Christocentricism into a Christomonism. There is only one plan of salvation—Protestant Evangelical theology (K. Barth and D. Bonhoeffer) has also worked this out very impressively—and this one plan of salvation, without any doubt, culminates in Jesus Christ. But one may not on this account disengage the reality of creation from Christ.

K. Rahner clearly outlined the Catholic position in these words: "*We* encounter this unsurpassed high point of history (the partnership with God) within the whole framework of our history—in which, already knowing something about man (and certainly also about God), we discover man—when we encounter Christ and therefore understand that he is a man. Theological anthropology would necessarily be curtailed if it were pursued exclusively from the standpoint of its goal, Christology; for the last experience does not cancel out the earlier one." [52] What is said here concerning the Christian understanding of man also holds for the Christian understanding of the world.

We say that the world, as created by God, has its self-subsistence, but the Logos entering into the reality of the world has taken its self-subsistence upon himself. World remains world; it is only truly released to its own reality through Christ, but it remains thereby indissolubly united to him. This fact is plain to see throughout history in the Church and will be brought to fruition in the second coming of Christ. The relationship of the world to the Church and its relationship to its perfected form in glory are no new levels in the relativity of the inherent value of earthly realities; they are only the unfolding and realization of that relativity to Christ the Head.

The third level of the relative intrinsic value of earthly realities is their relationship to the Church

a) The Church is in *its essence* a sign that man and world have been embraced by God in Christ. Through the Church, Christ enthroned at the right of the Father guides throughout history the work of *anakephalaiosis*, taking possession of the world and man in his corporeality. The Church is where the meaning of Christ for man and the world is preached, represented and made fruitful.

b) The most effective way in which this occurs is through the sacraments, especially the Eucharist. Here the union of all things in Christ is proclaimed and sacramentally realized. In the Eucharist, the cosmic-human association, founded in creation and exalted in the incarnation to brotherhood in Christ, progressively reaches reality. Its final form of realization is proclaimed until Christ comes again, but it also displays its hidden, powerful dynamism in the movement of history.

Mankind as a whole as well as its individual communities has within itself a natural ontological propensity toward the Eucharist. Thus he who in faith, hope and charity attends to the immanent dynamism and intentionality of the natural orders is from his very nature impelled, so to speak, to the mystery of the Eucharist.

A similar situation prevails in the material world, equally whether it directly constitutes the "body" of man or indirectly stands in his life and makes up his "world": in the Eucharist the bodily and worldly existence of man also comes to fulfilment. Just as the eternal Word at the incarnation united himself to a human body, so the *Kyrios* in the Eucharist unites himself to bread and wine. The eucharistic elements are exponents of the reality of the world in the same way that Jesus' human nature was in his time. In the Eucharist, the world is on the road to its fulfilment.

c) The *principles* for the concrete realization of the relationship of the Church and worldly orders were laid down by the Council of Chalcedon in 451. The Council, of course, spoke explicitly only of the relation between the two natures in Christ: his divine and human natures exist with one another not only without separation and division, but also without confusion and change, so that the distinction of the two natures is not abrogated by their union, but rather the individuality of each nature remains intact.[53]

This doctrinal statement, however, is valid not just for Christ as the head, but also for the Church as his body. The Church is truly the continuing presence of the God-man in history. If the Christological doctrine of the Council of Chalcedon is taken in an ecclesiological sense, it means that the Church and the world exist not only without separation and division, but also without confusion and change, so that the distinction of both orders is not abrogated by their union, but rather the individuality of each order remains intact. In other words, by the relationship of Church and world is meant the *principles of duality and integration*.

The principle of duality expresses nothing other than what we meant when we said that the world is self-subsistent and has its own proper worth and laws. When the "theology of earthly realities" provides for the liberation of the worldly orders to their own reality, it draws from the central mystery of Christology. Christ entrusts these worldly orders—which are also directed toward him—to their stewards and trustees directly, and not through the Church (the two-sword theory). The law of duality between the spiritual and temporal orders is valid for the entire duration of salvation history.

But the law of integration also prevails: the world is ordained to the Church, because here it is provided with salvation. The Church is where Christ effects the consummation of the world. Through the Church he takes the totality of the material and spiritual world, its being and its history, ever deeper into himself and fulfils it ever more forcefully with the power of salvation. Through the Church it remains evident that the inner-worldly realities can find no sufficiency in themselves, but rather, in order to be completed, must remain open to the kingdom of Christ.

The fourth level of the relative intrinsic value of earthly realities is finally their relationship to their perfected form

This perfected form is operative since the beginning as an entelechial dynamism. Its designation in creation was taken on by Christ, and proclaimed and realized in the Church through the Eucharist with increasing intensity. The Lord in his second coming will bring to fruition everything that he incorporated—or, to be more theologically cautious, ordered—to himself in the incarnation: thus the universal, evolving world of men and things which stretches out over all of history.

What we call "eternal life" will have the form of a community, and will "happen" in a corporeal manner in a transfigured cosmos. This is irrevocably pre-formed in the God-man, from the incarnation to the ascension. The human nature of Jesus has kept its individual being and is not tarnished in the light of glory. The dogma of Chalcedon safeguards also the eschatological truths about man and world. The world will indeed perish. It will not evolve ever more sublimely into a historical infinity. It will not forever experience in an eternal cycle new deaths and new births. It will be annihilated, but it will not remain in annihilation. Its materiality, as a new bodiliness and new worldliness, will be converted into a state of perfect glory and will here find eternal existence.

The eternal life will be the city of God in which the elect dwell together in love and peace, in opulence and splendor. It will be the banquet community which unites all with God and with one another; the kingdom in which the enthroned Lord exercises his dominion; the everlasting marriage feast of the lamb with mankind in a transformed world. Duality yet integration, being its own yet belonging to Christ—these will all be consummated.

This is the basic outline of a theology of earthly realities: In the Word, world and man are placed in existence; in the incarnation of the Word, they are given a direction. In the "fullness of time" the Word made flesh incorporated everything created into himself, in order to free it from the servitude of evil by his death and resurrection and lead it into the inner life of God. In the Church this work of the God-man is made present throughout time until it is brought to revealed and perfected glory in the parousia and handed over to the Father. Then God will be "all in all."

NOTES

[1] H. R. Schlette, *Die Nichtigkeit der Welt. Der philosophische Horizont des Hugo von St. Viktor* (Munich: 1961), p. 9.

[2] H. R. Schlette, "Welt" in: *Handbuch Theologischer Grundbegriffe II* (Munich: 1963), p. 826.

[3] Cf. H. Conrad-Martius, *Metaphysische Gespräche* (Halle: 1921), p. 113; A. Auer, *Weltoffener Christ* (3rd ed.; Düsseldorf: 1963), p. 43.

[4] Cf. the not-yet-published work of H. Hergenröther, *Die christliche Weltverachtung nach der De-contemptu-mundi Literatur von Ambrosius bis Erasmus*, pp. 59–89, where much material on this subject has been compiled; also, H. R. Schlette, *Die Nichtigkeit der Welt*, p. 163 f.

[5] "Magnanimité. L'idéal de la grandeur dans la philosophie païenne et dans la théologie chrétienne," *Bibliothèque thomiste* 28 (Paris: 1951), p. 496. For a treatment of the whole problem, cf. A. Auer, *op. cit.*, pp. 30–42.

[6] R. Guardini, *Das Ende der Neuzeit* (3rd ed.; Würzburg: 1951), p. 27. (Eng. tr.: *The End of the Modern World*: New York.) The medieval *Summas* seem strange to the modern spirit "until this spirit grasps what the medieval *Summas* really wanted to do: not an empirical research or rational elucidation of the world, but rather a construction of the 'world' from the content of revelation on the one hand, and from the principles and insights of ancient philosophy on the other. The *Summas* contain a world which has been erected in the mind, the whole of which can be compared with the endless differentiation and splendid unity of a cathedral . . ."

[7] Cf. A. Auer, *op. cit.*, pp. 44–48; and for what follows, H. Hergenröther, *op. cit.*

[8] "All is vanity."

[9] "Do not love the world or the things that are in the world . . . because all that is in the world is the lust of the flesh, and the lust of the eyes, and the pride of life; which is not from the Father, but from the world."

[10] H. Hergenröther, *op. cit.*, pp. 287–320, convincingly shows that this attitude was the strongest motive of the medieval contempt for the world.

[11] H. R. Schlette, *Die Nichtigkeit der Welt*, p. 35.

[12] *Ibid.*, p. 103. For Hugo of St. Victor, "the result of this practical understanding of the world is formally and materially equivalent to a basic dualism."

[13] R. Guardini, *op. cit.*, p. 34. H. R. Schlette, *Die Nichtigkeit der Welt*, pp. 80, 100, 160, in reference to K. Rahner on the "phenomenon of oblivion in the philosophy of religion," explains that the Middle Ages, especially Hugo of St. Victor, was permeated by an overwhelmingly dualistic conception of the world; this was so despite the fact that it could have come to a more positive outlook as a result of the theological groundwork (creation, redemption, consummation of the world). It is a fact that important theological truths are sometimes misunderstood or forgotten, although they are still handed on in dogma. "Despite the dogmatic correctness of the content of the Christian faith, in practical life and in the world-understanding an existential way of life may prevail, which—under Gnostic or Neo-Platonic influence—may totally deny this life and world and prefer that they did not exist at all." The question is this: whether the basic theological truths were ever held so lively in consciousness that one looking back at the Middle Ages can speak of "oblivion."

[14] R. Guardini, *op. cit.*, p. 55; cf. for what follows from p. 48 ff.; see also R. Guardini, *Welt und Person* (5th ed.; Würzburg: 1962), pp. 19–22.

[15] This turning point is visible in Petrarch, "the first modern man." Man no longer relates his experiences to God or mankind around him, but rather to himself; he is satisfied with the experience of himself. The starting point for the interpretation of life is no longer salvation history but the psychic experience. Regarding this self-experience of man according to Petrarch, cf. B. Groetuysen, *Philosophische Anthropologie* (Munich-Berlin: 1928), pp. 99–107.

[16] Cf. K. Popper, "Selbstbefreiung durch Wissen," in: *Der Sinn der Geschichte*, ed. L. Reinisch (2nd ed.; Munich: 1961), pp. 100–116. Instead of looking for a hidden meaning in history, we must give a meaning to history. We must agree with K. Popper, inasmuch as he is opposed to a prognosis of progress, a cyclic prognosis, one of destruction, and so forth. The fact that we ourselves give a meaning to history can imply that we ask ourselves: "What goals of political world history are worthy of man as well as politically possible?" (p. 102). Here also we

must agree with the author. But he does not pose the question whether a meaning for salvation history unfolds itself behind everything in world history. This is the author's perfect right, but theology has a right and a duty to pursue this inquiry.

[17] C. H. Ratschow, "Säkularismus," in: *Die Religion in Geschichte und Gegenwart V* (Tübingen: 1961), p. 1288.

[18] R. Guardini, *Das Ende der Neuzeit*, pp. 67–105.

[19] C. H. Ratschow, *op. cit.*, p. 1294. On p. 1293 the author ascertains that the specific point about this technocratic form of secularism is the "autonomy of an objective and calculable set of laws all its own ... which comprise and have the last word on everything about life as world and self and as nature and history." Cf. also J. Hommes, "Naturrecht, Person, Materie—das Anliegen der Dialektik," in: *Gesellschaft, Staat, Wirtschaft*, ed. J. Höffner, A. Verdross, F. Vito (Innsbruck-Vienna-Munich: 1961), esp. pp. 65–69, where it is philosophically shown how, at the apex of the modern profaneness, in the "absolute dialectic" not only the reality of nature, but also the reality of man in control of nature falls apart and disappears.

[20] C. H. Ratschow, *op. cit.*, pp. 1288–96.

[21] C. H. Ratschow is of the opinion that the Reformers' systematic clarification of the Middle Ages resulted in "a positive conclusion and faithful recapitulation." Through the teachings of the three classes, the two kingdoms and the *usus politicus legis*—thought patterns which have since become foreign to us—Luther determined the relationship of faith and the worldliness of the world in a novel and positive way. He could stress the worldliness of the world without impairing the majesty of God.

[22] R. Guardini, *Welt und Person,* p. 35: "The term 'coming of age' [*Mündigkeit*] does not mean anything ethical, but refers rather to the fact of advanced time, of greater age. A man is of age [*mündig*] in comparison to a boy. This does not mean that he is morally better, but that he sees the world more penetratingly, feels its reality more keenly, has a better idea of the potentialities and limits of his power, and a more distinct consciousness of his responsibility ... A corresponding phenomenon is found here. The modern man is of age in comparison to his medieval forebear." Cf. *ibid.*, pp. 24–26, 86.

[23] J. B. Metz, "Weltverständnis im Glauben. Christliche Orientierung in der Weltlichkeit der Welt heute," in: *Geist und Leben* 35 (1962),

p. 175. [This article is translated in this present volume: "A Believer Looks at the World."]

[24] *Ibid.*, p. 175.

[25] K. Rahner, "Anthropologie (theologische)," in: *Lexikon für Theologie und Kirche I* (2nd ed.; 1957), p. 622, speaks of a *"dei"* (Greek, meaning necessity), which, "from a historico-theological standpoint, is to be expected."

[26] G. Ebeling, "Die nicht-religiöse Interpretation biblischer Begriffe," in: *Zeitschrift für Theologie und Kirche* 52 (1955), pp. 296–360, shows how difficult and stratified the problems are. The discussion in Evangelical Protestant theology shows a great freedom and radicalism, which probably go together with the fact that the concepts of religion and church have here taken on a considerably less impervious and stabilized meaning than in Catholicism.

[27] *Ibid.*, p. 334. G. Ebeling much more profoundly develops D. Bonhoeffer's concept of the paradoxical conformity between the Christian faith and the process of radical secularization. We cannot, however, go into this any further here.

[28] *Ibid.*, p. 333. The author says more cautiously: "In regard to the phenomenon of religion, we encounter something simply unknown."

[29] H. Fries, "Die Botschaft von Christus in einer Welt ohne Gott," in: *Verkündigung und Glaube,* ed. Th. Filthaut and J. A. Jungmann (Freiburg i. Br.: 1958), pp. 100–122, gives a critical explanation of D. Bonhoeffer's theses concerning the coming of age of the world, the concept of religion, the realization of salvation through the crucifixion alone, and so forth.

[30] Cf. G. Ebeling, *op. cit.*, pp. 304–40. The works of D. Bonhoeffer which are especially important for our problem are: *Ethik,* ed. E. Bethge (3rd ed.; Munich: 1956) and *Widerstand und Ergebung,* ed. E. Bethge (7th ed.; Munich: 1956).

[31] Cf. W. Hartmann, "Säkularisierung," in: *Evangelisches Kirchenlexikon* III, pp. 768–73.

[32] Cf. F. Gogarten, *Verhängnis und Hoffnung der Neuzeit. Die Säkularisierung als theologisches Problem* (Stuttgart: 1953).

[33] Cf. H. Schreiner, *Die Säkularisierung als Grundproblem der deutschen Kultur* (publication of the Kirchlich–sozialen Bundes 73) (Berlin-

Spandau: 1930). Some good surveys of this discussion in Evangelicial Protestant theology are made by C. H. Ratschow, *op. cit.*, pp. 1288–96 and W. Hartmann, *op. cit.*, pp. 768–73.

[34] Cf. H. Kraemer, "Säkularismus," in: *Evangelisches Kirchenlexikon* III, pp. 773–76. Further literature: W. Hahn, "Säkularisation und Religionszerfall. Eine religions-psychologische Überlegung," in: *Kerygma und Dogma* 5 (1959), pp. 83–98, in which the author asks whether Western secularization implies a falling away from religion; F. Delikat, *Über den Begriff der Säkularisation* (Heidelberg: 1958), which contains an accurate research into the theological definition of the concept of secularization; M. Stallmann, "Was ist Säkularisierung?" in: *Sammlung gemeinverständlicher Vorträge und Schriften aus dem Gebiet der Theologie und Religionsgeschichte*, 227/228 (Tübingen: 1960), in which an introduction tracing the history of this concept is followed by a presentation of D. Bonhoeffer's and F. Gogarten's understanding of secularization.

[35] Cf. *Lexikon für Theologie und Kirche* I (2nd ed.; Freiburg: 1957), p. 623.

[36] F. v. Hügel, "Andacht zur Wirklichkeit," in: *Schriften in Auswahl*, selected, translated and introduced by M. Schlüter-Hermkes (Munich: 1952), p. 45.

[37] Inasmuch as Greek thought had already explored "being," it was itself already on the way to surmounting the "absolute" cosmos. This thought is developed by W. Weymann-Weyhe in an unpublished manuscript from a radio broadcast in 1962: *Die Welt ist nicht immer die gleiche. Kosmos, Naturgesetz, Wahrheit und Theologie*, pp. 15–19. This contribution is stimulating in many other respects as well.

[38] *Ibid.*, pp. 25–38.

[39] Cf. A. Mitterer, "Die Weltherrschaft des Menschen als Naturrecht," in: *Naturordnung in Gesellschaft, Staat, Wirtschaft* (Innsbruck-Vienna-Munich: 1961), pp. 44–47.

[40] Cf. A. Auer, *op. cit.*, pp. 270–76; also A. Auer, "Kirche und Welt," in: *Mysterium Kirche*, ed. F. Holböck, Th. Sartory (Salzburg: 1962), pp. 509–11.

[41] *Quadragesimo anno*: ". . . non iis quidem, quae artis sunt, sed in iis omnibus quae ad regulam morum referuntur." Herder edition (1931), p. 32.

[42] *Ibid.*: ". . . oeconomica res et moralis disciplina in suo quaeque ambitu suis utuntur principiis."

[43] O. v. Nell-Breuning, *Die soziale Enzyklika* (3rd ed.; Cologne: 1950), p. 60. Cf. also his important treatment of the ethics of economics as "institutional ethics" in the article "Zur Wirtschaftordnung," in: *Wörterbuch der Politik IV*, ed. O. v. Nell-Breuning, H. Sacher (Freiburg i. Br.: 1949), pp. 274–80.

[44] K. Rahner, *op. cit.*, p. 620.

[45] K. Löwith, "Der Weltbegriff der neuzeitlichen Philosophie," in: *Sitzungsberichte der Heidelberger Akademie der Wissenschaften, Phil.-Hist. Klasse IV* (Heidelberg: 1960), p. 9.

[46] J. B. Metz, *Christliche Anthropozentrik. Über die Denkform des Thomas von Aquin* (Munich: 1962), pp. 41–95, esp. pp. 41–51. According to W. Weymann-Weyhe, *op. cit.*, pp. 34–39, modern physics (C. F. von Weizäcker, W. Heisenberg) is drawing nearer to this Thomistic conception, insofar as all being is taken into the thinking spirit and only here becomes itself.

[47] J. Hommes, *op. cit.*, p. 64. For the whole picture cf. pp. 60–64.

[48] Cf. L. Scheffczyk, "Die Idee der Einheit von Schöpfung und Erlösung in ihrer theologischen Bedeutung," in: *Theol. Quartalschrift* 140 (1960), pp. 19–37.

[49] J. Danielou, *Vom Geheimnis der Geschichte* (Stuttgart: 1955), pp. 97 f. (Eng. tr.: *The Lord of History*: Chicago: 1958).

[50] Here is not the place to examine—even if it could be explained—what specific value is to be attached to the individual events of salvation: incarnation, death, resurrection, ascension.

[51] Cf. O. Karrer in a discussion regarding Teilhard de Chardin: *Christlicher Sonntag* 13 (1961). In his book *The Phenomenon of Man*, Teilhard calls the cosmos the "body of him who is and is coming"; in his hymn to matter, he calls it the "flesh of Christ." Cf. the recent, illuminating article by L. Scheffczyk, "Der *Sonnengesang* des hl. Franziskus von Assisi und die *Hymne an die Materie* des Teilhard de Chardin. Ein Vergleich zur Deutung der Struktur christlicher Schöpfungsfrömmigkeit," in: *Geist und Leben* 35 (1962), pp. 219–33.

[52] K. Rahner, *op. cit.*, p. 626 f.

[53] Denz. 148.

World History and Salvation History

by KARL RAHNER, S.J.

So MANY QUESTIONS and concerns are covered by the subject of world history and salvation-history that we could not possibly deal with them all. From within this vast field we have selected a few questions which seem of some importance to a Catholic theologian. We will formulate what can be said about them in a few quite simple theses, which we will then attempt to clarify.

1. Salvation-history takes place within the history of this world. Salvation is indeed what finally brings the whole man to his perfection; salvation can ultimately be granted to him by God alone. Salvation is not yet achieved and at best must yet become. It is impossible simply to encounter this salvation somewhere in the world. Indeed, it would be an absolutely fundamental heresy for any already given condition in the world, or any condition which man himself can realize by his own planning and action, to be regarded by him as his salvation, i.e., as what is really meant by salvation: the final and the beatifying.

Salvation, understood as an absolutely transcendent mystery—as that which comes from God and is outside our control—is one of the most basic concepts of Christianity. Accomplished salvation is in no sense a moment in history but rather the culminating cessation of history. It is not an object of possession or a produced effect but rather an object of faith, hope and prayer. By this fact alone, all utopian conceptions of salvation-in-this-world are to be rejected as doctrines meriting condemnation. History is by this fact declared to be the realm of the provisional, the unfinished, the ambiguous, the dialectical—and any attempt to seize salvation in this world and to find completion in the history of the world as such would itself remain a moment in history—part of what is evil, godless and vain in history—and would itself give way to other history coming after it.

And yet a Catholic-Christian theology of history cannot but say that salvation-history takes place within the history of the world. This means several things. First of all, salvation for the Christian is not a future which is simply still to come and which has not yet started at all since, when it does come, it will absorb the history of the world into itself. No, salvation takes place now. Man receives God's grace in the sense that grace is something which is already given to him now, something which he accepts and something which changes him interiorly. And since this grace is basically God communicating himself to man, it is not merely something provisional, nor is it merely a means to salvation nor a substitute for salvation. Grace is really this salvation itself, for it is God himself in his forgiving and divinizing love.

Salvation-history within the history of the world means further that this self-communication of God—which is the communication of salvation as such—takes place in the form of that free acceptance of this communication which we call faith, hope and charity in the freedom of man. And man's free surrender of himself to God who communicates himself to him is not merely an esoterically confined happening in the life of man. Of course, since faith is meant to include all human dimensions in this salvation—so that nothing in man may stand unrelated outside of salvation—this faith (by which salvation is accepted) may and must indeed render itself consciously and socially tangible in the very ground of man's existence in his profession of faith, in worship and in the Church.

Yet this acceptance of salvation in freedom takes place just as much with reference to the material presuppositions of man's freedom in which that freedom is accomplished. Real freedom of the spirit, in this world of the God of grace and of Christ, is always freedom with regard to salvation or damnation and cannot be freedom in any other way. Yet precisely this freedom of the corporeal, social and historical creature which is man is always and necessarily a freedom which is exorcised through an encounter with the world—the community and environment in which man lives; its nature combines both that of transcendental freedom and of a particular category of freedom. Hence the freedom of acceptance or refusal of salvation occurs in all the dimensions of human existence, and it occurs always in an encounter with the world and not merely in the confined sector of the sacred or of worship and "religion" in the narrow sense; it occurs in encounters with one's neighbor, with one's historical task, with the so-called world of everyday life, in and with what we call the history of the individual and of communities.

Salvation-history thus takes place right in the midst of ordinary history. Man works out his salvation or damnation in everything he does and in everything which impels him. Everything in the history of the world is pregnant with eternity and eternal life or with eternal ruin.

There is yet a third factor to be brought out with regard to this inclusion of salvation-history within profane history—a factor which is more characteristic of the Catholic understanding of this relationship than the first two we have mentioned. As we will state at much greater length later, the content and reality proper to salvation-history do indeed lie hidden in profane history, since immediately tangible historical events and realities do not of themselves give us any clear clue—they can be of a saving or a damning nature. These events and realities do not of themselves betray whether here and now something saving or damning is taking place in them.

Yet this concealment of salvation-history in an ambiguous and undefined profane history which cannot be simply interpreted or "judged" as a saving history, does not mean that salvation-history is enacted solely in an individual, transempirical history of the individual existent of conscious and of absolutely intangible faith. It does not mean that salvation-history takes place behind a profane history which goes its own quiet way and is quite indifferent to it, simply in the form of a supra-history or history of faith. It is true that profane history in *general* and on the *whole* is ambiguous and cannot of its nature be interpreted with absolute certainty in questions about what part of it is salvation and what damnation. Profane history will reveal itself clearly in this respect only in the Last Judgment, which itself is not a moment of history but rather the final unveiling of history.

But all this does not mean that profane history does not become transparent here and there and does not within its own sphere on occasion draw man's attention by signs and references to the question of faith and salvation and orientate the answer to this question in a particular direction. Salvation-history, which of its nature is a hidden history, works itself out in the dimension of profane history in which it takes place. God, who grants salvation, addresses man within the profane dimension of history. He does this through the prophets who interpret the inward history of grace and revelation by their words, giving it a socially tangible form and authenticating this by those empirical facts, called miracles, which precede faith and justify it in a this-worldly manner before reason and moral responsibility, even though they cannot and are not intended to produce this faith.

But above all, the history of this world has become transparent with respect to salvation (in a way which cannot be surpassed in this world) through the Christ-event in Jesus of Nazareth—through his resurrection and by the proof of the Spirit bestowed by him. In other words, the same man who in his whole and entire being is faced with the decision concerning salvation in his historical existence, has ultimately only one history, in the sense that there are no isolated sectors of his existence which are in no way codetermined by the history of grace and faith (or vice versa). And this one history is not so uniform and homogeneous as to make salvation and God's action always and universally so clearly present in it that a profane zone of history could no longer be experienced at all or that the genuine decision of faith would no longer be possible; for if this were the case, then no matter where man turned in such a history, he could not avoid encountering God and his offer of salvation everywhere with equal inevitability.

In all this it can be left an open question here as to whether the eyes of faith alone can see this salvation-history shining through profane history in such a way that it is also accepted. In any case, the whole of profane history is disturbing, reproachful and disappointing even in its own sphere, and anyone who asks for salvation and reckons with the possibility of a personal self-exposure will find that profane history contains hints and "signs" telling him where this salvation has taken place in his own history and where it is to be found. Salvation-history takes place within profane history.

2. Salvation-history is distinct from profane history. We have already had to enunciate this second thesis in explanation of the first. We must now reflect more explicitly and exactly on it.

a) Salvation-history is distinct from profane history, first, because profane history by and large does not permit of any unequivocal interpretation with respect to the salvation or damnation taking place within it. Salvation and damnation are events of profane history, for wherever men achieve themselves in freedom they stand before God and decide their salvation. If this were not so, then their activity would not be free in the real metaphysical and theological sense. For freedom means man's self-determination in the face of God, whether he actually understands it explicitly in this way or not. But this saving or damning characteristic of the historical, free decisions of man remains hidden. It does not of itself become a historically tangible fact. For a free action becomes "historical" in the strict sense only once it is objectified in such a way as to be explicitly expressed in words as an object of human intercommunication in the various forms of the objective spirit in science, art, society, etc. Of itself, however, the saving or damning character of a free human act cannot become objectified, and therefore historical, in this sense.

This is impossible for several reasons. The ultimate quality of freedom cannot become the object of reflection. For the motives—adopted in freedom and accepted as effective motives—which determine the moral and religious quality of freedom are not simply identical with the conscious motives adopted in their conceptual explicitness. Man always acts from a knowing and self-possessed basis of his freedom, a basis which cannot be accounted for simply by representational and moral reflection. For the content of consciousness is greater and wider, deeper and more original than the sum total of what is known. Even consequent reflection is itself again an act which—reflectively—cannot outstrip its own limits. By this token, therefore, every form of reflection itself is a merely provisional, inexact account which only approximates to the totality of the basis and motivation of freedom but never catches hold of it completely.

If this is true of the moral reflection of the individual subject of freedom on himself, it is a fortiori true also of the objectifications of his moral decisions in words, purporting to communicate him to others, as well as in the various forms of the objective spirit. It is undoubtedly possible to recognize in many cases, with sufficient certainty, whether these objectifications are in accord with an objective moral norm or not. But it is impossible to derive any real certainty from them about the moral quality of the innermost free decision a person makes with respect to God. And hence it is also impossible to do this with respect to the question of whether this or that historical act is an event of salvation or damnation. By looking at the reality of history as it offers itself to reflection and objectifies itself in word and deed and only thus becomes historical in the strictest sense, one can surmise, hope or fear—but one cannot judge. The history of the world is not itself the judgment of the world, no matter how true it is that this judgment really takes place in that history.

Furthermore, salvation is not to be found in the finality of the free decision of man, if this is taken to mean that man simply creates this salvation himself by his free decision. Salvation is God communicating himself—it is his free act, which is God himself—since there is no salvation in the real order apart from God himself. This God, in his free communication of himself, in the grace-giving gift of his own eternal glory, must indeed be accepted in freedom, even though this acceptance is itself once more an act of that human freedom which in turn is a gift of God himself, granted to man by God's communication of himself. But the God who communicates himself can only be experienced in his own reality by a direct experience without the veil of faith covering up this reality. God's very own reality can only be experienced in the direct vision of God—in an event, in other words, which is the achievement and in that sense the cessation of history and not a moment in history—which is the fruit and not merely the maturing of that fruit.

For these two reasons, i.e., the freedom of man and the gift of salvation by God, the event of salvation is indeed contained and achieved in profane history and yet is not present historically in its quality of saving event as such but is rather believed or hoped for. By and large, profane history does not of itself offer us any certain interpretation about salvation or damnation. Man works out his history, and it pertains to the inscrutable counsels of God alone to judge this otherwise unjudged history. History carries its eternal content into the silent mystery—it itself cannot enjoy that content.

And this is the first aspect under which salvation-history and profane history are distinct.

b) If we were to regard salvation-history only from the viewpoint emphasized up to now, it would still always be coextensive with profane history, for the latter would then represent the undeciphered and indecipherable salvation-history. The only difference between salvation-history and profane history would then lie in the fact that the one is judged and the other is not. They would be formally but not materially distinct from each other. There is in fact a reality and concept of salvation-history and even revelation-history (and our first task now will have to be to work this out more clearly) which is not indeed formally identical in this sense, though materially coextensive, with the reality and concept of the profane history of the world.

And so, before we can work out a material difference between salvation- and revelation-history in the narrowest sense of the word and the history of the world, we must first of all consider—or rather emphasize more explicitly—this material identity of a general revelation- and salvation-history and the profane history of the world. It is part of the Catholic statement of faith that the supernatural saving purpose of God extends to all men in all ages and places in history. Everyone is offered salvation, which means that everyone, insofar as he does not close himself to this offer by his own free and grave guilt, is offered divine grace—and is offered it again and again (even when he is guilty).

Every man exists not only in an existential situation to which belongs the obligation of striving toward a supernatural goal of direct union with the absolute God in a direct vision, but also in a situation which presents the genuine subjective possibility of reaching this goal by accepting God's self-communication in grace and in glory. Because of God's universal saving purpose, the offer and possibility of salvation extend as far as the history of human freedom. But furthermore, this offer of the supernatural elevation of the spiritual reality of man, enabling him to move by his spiritual and personal dynamism toward the God of the supernatural beatifying life, is not merely an objective state of being in man which could be thought of simply as something beyond consciousness. Grace, being supernaturally divinizing, must rather be thought of as a change in the structure of human consciousness.

This does not necessarily nor always mean that consciousness is given new and proper objects which were until then unknown to it. But the "formal object" (as scholastic theology is in the habit of saying), the horizon within which the normal, empirically experienced realities of consciousness are grasped, and the ultimate orientation of consciousness are changed by grace. This supernatural horizon is not necessarily such that it could or ought to be made an object of reflection in itself or that it ought to be taken out of the context of and distinguished from the transcendental horizon (of the experience of being) natural to the intellectual consciousness of man. For there is no question here of an individual, changeable datum of consciousness but rather of the a priori horizon of consciousness—and this a priori formal horizon, within which the intellectual life of man is enacted, is always present in everyone.

This horizon is not as such an object, but an unobjectified horizon within which the spiritual existence of man takes place. Yet precisely as such, it is unsystematically and unreflectively and indeed for the greater part "unreflectably" conscious—conscious but not known. It is that inexpressible, nameless and—precisely as such —present ordination of man in knowledge and freedom to something which is beyond anything assignable, which does not declare itself as an individual object would but is as it were silent, and yet by that very fact is all the more all-embracing and operative in everything. It is the dynamism of the spirit's transcendence into the infinity of the silent mystery which we call God—the dynamism which is really meant to arrive and to accept, and not merely to be the eternally approaching but never quite arriving movement toward the infinity of God; it is meant to reach the infinity of God, since God gives himself to it of his own accord and in such a way that he has already even now entered freely into this movement of infinite transcendence itself as its innermost moving-force and raison d'être.

If this is so, then this supernatural elevation of man which is granted by God's universal saving purpose already has of itself the nature of a revelation. Of course, it is not of its own nature alone a revelation in the sense of a propositionally expressed communication about some particular, definite individual object. It is, however, a revelation in the sense of a change of consciousness (although not a change of knowledge), which originates from a free personal self-communication of God in grace. It is, therefore, absolutely legitimate to call it already a revelation, especially since it already communicates or offers in an ontologically real sense as "grace" something which also ultimately constitutes the whole content of divine revelation contained in proper propositions and human concepts, viz., God and his eternal life itself which, as God's self-communication in grace and glory, is the salvation of men. If man accepts this, his supernaturally elevated transcendence—this supernatural horizon and hence this divine revelation in the self-communication of the one revealed—then he exercises, even though as yet in a very unsystematic manner, what in a Christian sense can certainly be called faith.

It follows then that there is a history of salvation, revelation and faith which coexists with general profane history. We have called this the general salvation- and revelation-history so as to distinguish it from that other salvation- and revelation-history with which we will have to deal more explicitly in a moment. Of course, as we have already indicated briefly above, the notion of "history" contained in the concept of the general salvation- and revelation-history must be understood in a wide and (if you will) watered-down sense. We can call it a history of salvation and revelation because it is a matter of real decisions and free acts both on the part of God and on the part of man; it is a matter of mutual, personal communications which are performed concretely in and on the material of profane history.

But we can apply the term "history" to this general salvation- and revelation-history only in a wider sense. For strictly as such and by its a priori transcendental tendency, it does not as yet appear in those objectifications in word and objective cultural values which make it possible to have direct intercommunication between men, to have a concrete community of men and to have reflexly apprehensible knowledge about the relation to empirically experienced and communicable realities—and which in short represent history in the fullest sense of the word.

This does not mean, however, that the general salvation- and revelation-history belongs to an absolutely meta-empirical sphere which is in no way connected with the tangibility of normal history. The basic condition or horizon in the line of grace of which we have spoken and which is the foundation of the fact that there is a general salvation- and revelation-history at all times and even outside the Old and New Covenants, will make itself felt in the concrete history of men. It will influence the concrete forms of religion, of man's self-knowledge, of his philosophy and morality, even when this horizon as such cannot (or at least not easily) be made the object of reflection in conceptual purity and sureness of truth. There is a unity in the dimensions of human existence—the whole man is called to salvation—and there is an inner dynamism of grace by which it becomes effective in a healing, sanctifying and divinizing way in all the dimensions of man.

It is therefore to be expected, furthermore, that this divinized ground of man will everywhere and always (although with varying force and very differing success) try to become the object of reflection, driven to this by the very dynamism of grace under a supernatural, saving providence of God. It is to be expected that it will try to objectify itself in explicit expressions of religion, such as in the liturgy and religious associations, and in protests of a "prophetic" kind against any natural attempt by man to shut himself up in the world of his own categories and against any (ultimately polytheistic) misinterpretations of this basic grace-full experience.

We cannot in the present context go into the details of this interaction between profane history and general salvation- and revelation-history. But if this were possible, we could no doubt show that a Christian understanding of the universal saving purpose of God, and of the nature of supernatural grace, would enable us to gain a far more positive understanding of the explicit, reflex and socially constituted general history of religion which after all coexists with profane history.

This would show us that it is absolutely possible to conceive of a religion before Christianity even apart from the Old Covenant—a religion quite legitimate in the eyes of the saving providence of God, i.e., positively willed by providence even though it might inseparably contain certain elements not willed by God. Thus, the Old Testament (as against the New) might be conceived in many respects as a divinely interpreted model of pre-Christian religion rather than as an absolutely and in every respect unique and incomparable quality.

We must, however, pass over these considerations here, even though they would greatly contribute to the elucidation of the question about the relation between profane and saving history. We will therefore return now to the consideration of the question of why and in what respect salvation-history and profane history must be distinguished.

c) Salvation-history and profane history are distinct because God has interpreted a particular part of this profane and otherwise ambiguous history by his word (which is a constitutive element of salvation-history itself), by giving it a saving or damning character. Thus he has distinguished this particular part of the one history from the rest of history and has made it the actual, official and explicit history of salvation.

This explanation of the difference between the two histories may seem rather surprising at first. It may be thought that surely salvation-history in the strictest sense is to be found in the Old Testament and at the moment when Jesus Christ, the Word become flesh, came onto this earth, and when miracles occur—in brief, wherever God acts within history and accomplishes his actions on man.

Yet our thesis becomes immediately understandable if we ask ourselves about the reason for the presence of God's deeds in the history of men, and about the reason why God's actions enter into the properly historical dimension. For we still have to answer that it is through the word. A miracle would be merely an extraordinary and inexplicable event which would tell us nothing—even when, and precisely when, it refers to an empirically tangible and verifiable state of affairs—if it did not occur in connection with a word-revelation which is authenticated by it and which, in its turn, gives the miracle its basic meaning; the word-revelation makes the miracle basically comprehensible and gives point to its role as a sign indicating something.

To the extent to which the real historical content of the Old Testament is not uttered and does not consist of the Word itself, the Old Testament can quite properly be regarded as the natural saving providence of God or as God's saving providence intended for and accorded to all peoples. In other words, we can conceive God as Lord of a national history which becomes an event of salvation only once it is clearly interpreted by the word of the prophets as corresponding or contrary to the will of God. And with regard to Jesus Christ, his incarnation or hypostatic union is naturally a fact which is more than a human word; but it finds its inner, necessary and co-constitutive continuation in the absolute human consciousness in Jesus of being the Son of God—and it would not be present for us in our historical dimension (precisely because of its peculiar characteristic as an absolute transcendent mystery) without the self-revelation of Jesus in his human words.

Having said all this, we do not mean to maintain that salvation-history is nothing but the divine Word in human words. Such an assertion which would identify the history of salvation with that of faith and which would reduce the history of faith to a purely existential actualism is not intended by what we have said. What we do say, however, is that the saving acts of God as such become present in the dimension of human history—in other words, become themselves historical—only when the word which expresses and interprets them is added. This is therefore not a word added externally or subsequently, which is pronounced about something already tangibly present in the realm of human history even without it; rather, it is an inner constitutive element of God's saving activity considered as an event of human history as such.

Hence, wherever profane history is clearly interpreted by the word of God in history as to its saving or damning character—wherever God's actions in general salvation- and revelation-history are clearly and certainly objectified by the word of God—and wherever the absolute, unsurpassable and indissoluble unity of God and the world, and its history in Jesus Christ, become historically manifest by Christ's testimony to himself in the form of words—there is found the special, official history of salvation and revelation, immediately differentiated and standing out in relief from profane history.

For the interpreting and revealing word of God which constitutes the official and special revelation- and salvation-history as distinct from the general salvation- and revelation-history, does not occur always and everywhere but has its special place in time and space within history. Nor does it clearly interpret the saving or damning character of all early history but leaves large tracts of it unexplained, although it does provide rules of interpretation regarding this profane history (with which we will deal later) to aid the believing and hopeful ventures of the historically existing man.

This setting-into-relief of saving history from profane history has itself a history all its own. It has not been equally intense and clear in all ages. Nor could it be. For by the general history of grace, salvation and revelation, real salvific activity becomes coexistent with the history of the world and takes place within it at all times and everywhere. For this reason salvation-history is always the hidden foundation of profane history which also manifests itself in the latter in ever new forms: the religious element is everywhere the meaning and root of history and is never merely the most sublime flower of a merely human culture which is the word of men; it is already propelled from within by God-effected grace and codetermined from within by the proper, general salvation-history.

Wherever the latter reveals itself so clearly that it begins to become itself historically tangible in word and in the objectifications of the spirit of history, there the general salvation-history begins to pass over into special salvation-history: we do not know exactly whether this or that man is a religious thinker and a religiously creative man or already a prophet; we ask ourselves whether this or that religious experience is the mystical expression of man's search for infinite transcendence or already the mysticism of the experience of grace which carries the dynamic urge of the soul into the divine life; we are not quite sure whether this or that element of worship, religious institutionalization or custom is merely permitted, encouraged, or positively willed by God so that it may be the historical embodiment of that orientation toward God which is characteristic of the deepest reality of man and without which no one finds his salvation.

We know that the Old Testament as a whole, with its great men of God and with all that has objectified itself in the holy Scriptures of the Old Testament, has been acknowledged by God as something really willed by him and as his own preparation for salvation—in other words, we know that it was real salvation-history within and delimited from profane history. Yet in the Old Testament, too, the dividing line between saving and profane history is still very fluid: it was only with difficulty that men in O.T. times could distinguish between authentic and false prophets.

For the prophets appeared only sporadically, and there was as yet no institution which could act as a final court of appeal endowed with an absolute discernment of spirits which could have distinguished on every occasion between genuine prophets, legitimate religious renewal and criticism on the one hand, and false prophets and developments perversive of religion on the other. The Old Covenant, taken as a whole, could have fallen away from its mission and from being an authentic, official and historical tangible manifestation of the saving purpose of God for the people of Israel: it could have become an empty sign, an illegitimate usurpation of the sign of God's grace in the world.

Nor do we maintain that God did not make arrangements for the historically tangible salvation of other peoples, analogous to the arrangements of the Old Testament. Of course, it remains the privilege of Israel that its tangible and to some extent distinct salvation-history was the immediate historical prelude to the incarnation of the divine Word, and that this history of Israel alone was interpreted authoritatively by the word of God in Scripture in such a way that it was thereby distinguished from any other profane history (which also always contains religious elements), and that only thus it became the official and special salvation-history in distinction to profane history.

Only in Jesus Christ did the divine and the human reach an absolute and indissoluble unity; only in the self-revelation of Jesus is this unity also historically present; only now is this saving history clearly and permanently distinguished from all profane history; and everything, such as the Church, the sacraments and the Scriptures, which follows from this Christ-event and which participates in its own way in this unsurpassable finality of the Christ-event, participates also in its distinction from profane history. Here in Christ and in the Church, saving history reaches its clearest and absolutely permanent distinction from profane history and becomes really an unequivocally distinct manifestation within the history of the world, thus bringing the general salvation-history to self-realization and to its historical reality in word and social structures within the history of the world.

By this very fact, this distinct salvation-history of an explicitly verbal, social and sacramental kind is also something destined for all men of every future age. It intends to gather into itself the whole general salvation- and revelation-history and to represent it historically within itself; it *strives* therefore to coincide with the general salvation- and revelation-history and thus also with profane history, although it knows quite well that these two can never be fully identified in history but only in the culminating dissolution of history.

3. Salvation-history explains profane history. This is the third point we wish to make here about the subject under discussion. This statement means two things. First, salvation-history is an explanation of profane history because, in the form of general salvation-history, it represents the most profound character and the basis of profane history, and because, in the form of official and special salvation-history, it manifests this ultimate character of all history in the revelation in which salvation takes place and at the same time shows itself historically. Second, salvation-history presents us by its word with an interpretation of profane history. These two aspects of the above statement do not require separate consideration.

a) Salvation-history sets itself into relief from the history of the world—it demythologizes, undeifies the history of the world. Creation and history are not yet salvation. Salvation is God and his grace, and God's grace is not simply identical with the reality which is engaged in evolving history. Just as Christianity strips the world of divine attributes—first by showing that it has a created nature essentially distinct from God, and second by prohibiting any conception of the world which regards it simply as the corporeal aspect of the gods—so does history. History is not simply the history of God himself—a theogony—and therefore does not find its ultimate basis in itself and is not self-explanatory. History is not the judgment of the world but is something created, finite, temporal and essentially referred to the Mystery which is other than itself. The *Kronos* and *Ananke* of history are not gods.

Man has been cast into this undeified world. He does not merely live in salvation-history. He is a Christian and works out his salvation, doing this precisely by taking upon himself the soberness of the profane which is not yet itself salvation. Salvation-history creates its own presupposition by the very fact of turning the profane, the ambiguous, the God-veiling—in a word, the world and profane history—into the climate of faith and probation.

It is true that salvation-history is silent about profane history, leaving its questions open and letting the cockle grow with the wheat without trying to make any clear-cut distinction between them. There is a way in which Christianity declares itself incompetent with respect to worldly matters, the State and politics, economics, and other cultural affairs. At first sight, all this may appear to anyone who thinks he can deal with the world on his own as an all too desirable modesty. Yet in reality, this dualism between State and Church, science and theology—in short, between Christianity and the world together with its history—has another, quite different side to it. We refer to the fact that God leaves history to its own devices; he leaves it to journey into the indefinite, to make its own attempts, to be responsible for its own "planning," and he leaves it the possibility of losing its way and of tragically destroying itself, etc., even where people are not disobedient to the word of God and his commandments.

Salvation-history, therefore, tells anyone who is looking for salvation to go out into profane history too—this history which remains a dark, unexplained and incalculable task—and tells him to hold out there, to prove himself there, to believe that life has a meaning even though this remains unexplained, and precisely in this sense to accept God as his salvation. In short, salvation-history, by bringing out the distinction between profane history and itself, sends man out into a demythologized world which is not so much the realm of the rule of the gods, but rather the raw material for the task imposed on man—for the task which indeed man, the *homo faber*, actually and legitimately imposes on himself—only to know that, when he has fulfilled this task, he has still not gained salvation for himself by his own powers, but receives it as a gift from God, since it is more than the world and history.

b) Salvation-history interprets the history of the world as something antagonistic and veiled. Precisely because salvation is not simply the immanent fruit of profane history, Christianity is skeptical toward profane history. It lets man go out to his worldly task, because it is precisely in the obscurity and ambiguity of this earthly task that man must work out his salvation which is by faith. Yet for Christianity this very task in the world is something which will always remain unfinished and which will ultimately always again end in failure. For as far as the individual is concerned, this task always finds an absolute limit in death.

In the same way Christianity also shows that death is to be found even in the midst of universal history. This implies a futility arising from the fact that what can always be planned only partially will always remain incalculable—a futility which ever springs afresh out of man's evil heart, even over and above the inherent tragedy of everything finite. Christianity knows no history which would evolve of its own inner power into the kingdom of God itself, and it does not really matter whether one conceives this kingdom as the realm of the enlightened mind, or of the fully civilized man, or of the classless society, or in any other way whatsoever.

The opposition between man and woman, the intelligent and the stupid, the rich and the poor, war and peace, rulers and subjects, and any other ineradicable antitheses of existence may take different forms, may become more refined and more bearable; the effort to humanize these oppositions may even be a duty for the human race —one which is imposed on it and whose fulfilment is to a certain extent even forced upon it by the exigencies of history. Nevertheless, the oppositions will always remain; they will always weigh heavily on man and will always renew the pain and bitter melancholy of human existence.

Indeed, in Christian eschatology these terrestrial antitheses—this combat between light and darkness, good and evil, faith and unbelief—are known to take on ever acuter forms. Of course, this combat which is actually part and parcel of salvation-history will never be such that the human combatants engaged on either side of this fight would identify themselves or could be identified with absolute goodness or absolute evil. No one but God can ever distinguish these ultimate fronts of salvation-history adequately, for they will always cut through the parties engaged in these combats in the history of the world as well as the individuals concerned.

Yet according to Christian eschatology, the decisions taken in salvation-history will be enacted in ever clearer forms and signs; they will fashion their own embodiments and expressions in the most profound depths of existence within the history of the world, even though the final judgment, which will make a clear distinction between the wheat and the cockle within these objectifications, belongs to God alone.

Christianity denies that the history of the world is progressing toward eternal peace—although this does not mean that war, which will always be with us, must necessarily be fought with halberds or atomic bombs. Christianity knows that all progress in profane history is also another step toward the possibility of greater dangers and ultimate ruin. History will never be the place for eternal peace and shadowless light; rather, if this life is measured by the absolute demands which God has empowered man to make, or indeed which man has a God-given duty to make, it will always be the land of death and darkness.

c) The history of the world is an existentially devaluated (*depotenzierte*) history in its Christian interpretation. We must be careful in our evaluation of profane history. The Christian is certainly not one who has such a merely private interest in his salvation that he can settle down in some dead corner of the history of the world and seek his salvation there—quite unconcerned about the passage of the history of the world—in a flight from the world which in the last analysis is quite impossible.

It may be winter in the history of a people or in some other kind of historical form. It may be impossible in some particular period of history to achieve anything lofty or great, things to which one would otherwise be bound in duty. A man may perhaps even recognize this and *hence* know himself to be released from such a duty. There may be quite legitimate withdrawals from public life, from politics and the market place of an impoverished age; indeed, in certain periods this may be the only possible way of existing for a wise, honest and courageous person, for not even he is capable of everything, nor is he bound to consider himself capable of it.

Yet all this does not mean that the Christian may in principle withdraw from history. He has a duty toward history, he must make and suffer history. He can find the eternal only in the temporal. Yet this again does not mean that the temporal and the eternal are simply the same. And to this extent the Christian has both the right and the duty to make history something relative and—in a true sense —to devaluate and disarm it existentially.

Who shall separate us from the love of Christ? Shall tribulation, or distress, or persecution, or hunger or nakedness, or danger or the sword? I am sure that neither death, nor life, nor angels, nor principalities, nor powers, nor things present, nor things to come, nor height nor depth, nor any other creature will be able to separate us from the love of God, which is in Christ Jesus our Lord—says St. Paul. But this means that every significance proper to the history of the world is always already outdated for us, not indeed on our account but on account of God in Christ—always presupposing that we have taken refuge by faith in this outmoding of history by God in Christ. Neither death nor life, neither things present nor future possibilities are the ultimate, the finally significant, that which is salvation.

Hence the Christian is told over and over again with respect to the history of this world and its incalculable possibilities and tasks: what does it profit a man if he gain the whole world but suffer the loss of his own soul? *This* flight from the world, which sees the significance of empirical history as something relative, is part of what is meant by being a Christian. It is no stoic ataraxy, no cowardice or cynicism. It is the faith which knows that entry into God's eternity can be gained through all the exits of the history of the world and through every rise or fall, provided only that one accepts God's salvation in faith—which one can do under any of the forms of profane history.

That which often seems to be a somewhat narrow-minded, self-centered anxiety about salvation in the life of the Christian—this attitude of someone's trying to salvage his soul out of the chaos of the times—is in fact (wherever it is the action of a true Christian) the attitude of a magnificent superiority of the faith over the world, such as is given expression in the text of St. Paul quoted above. It means that the true Christian can take history seriously because he knows it to be already overcome by Christ. The history of this world is devalued in a Christian sense, because salvation can take place in all its most contradictory forms; and at the same time this history is increased in value since in it can truly take place the limitless salvation, the eternal and lasting salvation which is God himself.

d) For Christianity, the history of this world is a history interpreted in a Christocentric sense. This is really just a summary of what we have been saying. The world is the world created for the eternal Logos—by him and for him. The world and its history have been designed from the very beginning with a view to the Word of God become flesh. Since God wished, because he is Love, to express himself in his eternal Word, the world exists, and exists complete with the difference between nature and grace, and thus between salvation-history and profane history. For this very reason this means that this difference is enveloped by Christ and by God's absolute self-expression which takes place in Christ.

Hence the history of the world too—and precisely in its profane nature—is a part of the pre- and post-history of Christ. Natural history in its material content and in its living form is the sphere which God puts before the finite spirit as the condition of its possibility—as the presupposition which transcends itself into the realm of the finite spirit by the dynamism of the absolute Spirit. So also the totality of the history of the world is the presupposition God has provided for salvation-history as the condition of its possibility transcending itself into it.

Thus the history of the world is the sphere and the pre-history of the history of Christ, which is, since he is engaged in history not indeed as someone who needs to be but as the Love who surrenders himself, the history of God himself. That, however, which embraces world- and salvation-history in their unity and diversity, is the most real history of all.

A Believer's Look at the World

A Christian Standpoint in the Secularized World of Today[1]

by JOHANNES B. METZ

I. A SUGGESTION FOR A CHRISTIAN'S WORLD-VIEW TODAY

THE WORLD TODAY has become secular, and—unless all appearances are deceptive—the end of the secularization is by no means in sight.[2] This universal secularism puts the challenge fairly and squarely: what should the attitude of faith be in this situation? Faith can, of course, attempt to curtain itself off from such an uncomfortable state of affairs, to keep presuming from behind closed doors the well-tried formulas of theology and piety—just as though the day of Pentecost had not yet dawned, and with it the need to understand and provide an answer for each successive age.

This sort of timeless faith at least avoids embarrassment from within, that salutary embarrassment which comes from God and through which God opens new paths. Such a faith is never at a loss for words; it can talk about God and the world with astonishing complacency. But all too noticeably it lacks the ring of the true answer required, the color of reality; in the very heart of Christendom it slips unaware to the level of a mythology.

But if the theologian faces up to the situation which confronts him—and it is his inability to turn a blind eye to this situation which, in the last analysis, spells out God's irresistible challenge—then perhaps the first thing he sees is how thin and poverty-stricken are his words and his notions. Perspectives accepted for many a year fall away; ground in which he has trusted all too much opens before his feet. He must take up a position in the almost unexplored possibility of existence in faith.

Certainly attempts are being made today to provide an answer in the spirit of revelation and theology to the world situation which confronts us. These attempts merit respect; we cannot describe and evaluate them here. One attempt is to insert the secularism of our world today into a "theology of earthly realities," in that immediacy of God which was a commonplace of the medieval world-picture.[3] Another is to inculcate in the Christian an unprejudiced "openness to the world," with the clear goal and object of assimilating this secular world and giving it new roots in the mystery of Christ.[4] But both of these seem to us anachronistic attempts to restore the past.

We also wonder whether the thoroughly justified stress of Christian "openness," according to which the world appears as the immediate material of the Christian's activity, takes fully into account the character of the secularism in question. For it is highly varied and complicated, scarcely admitting of total comprehension or full penetration, springing as it does from so many factors. Does not this world picture come perilously close to an optimism about the world which breeds a Christian disquiet precisely in the man who really takes this secularism seriously?

Be that as it may, at this point we would merely like to point out that this and all such attempts have one feature in common: they all take more or less for granted that this secularism *as such* is something fundamentally contrary to a Christian understanding of the world, and must therefore be totally overcome by Christianity. They all share the *basic* rejection of the concrete process of secularization begun in recent ages and sharply expressed in our contemporary world situation.[5]

It is precisely this "obvious" presumption which seems to us to be questionable in the light of the theology of history. For a theology which thinks historically cannot easily be content to take refuge in the claim that this modern secularization is at heart unchristian and that for this reason world-history has again developed decisively away from salvation-history. In such a concept there lurks a dangerously extrinsic approach to salvation-history as well as a positivist approach to theology which does not take completely seriously the truth that the "spirit" of Christianity is permanently incorporated in the "flesh" of world-history, in whose irreversible march it must make itself felt and play a decisive part.

Theology cannot facilitate its task by neglecting the actual process of world-history in the way a Monophysitic approach to salvation-history does. No, world-history is and remains that which is taken up into the Christian Logos; it can never again decisively fall away. Theology has the duty to track and show forth this wedding —always hidden and crucified, but none the less permanent—between world-history and salvation-history. In relation to our present problem, theology must bring out the fact that, and the way in which, the Christian starting point has not just disappeared from view, but still remains effective in the historically irreversible and decisive event of modern secularization.

We may not disregard this process; we cannot take it seriously enough. But how does it fit under the domination of the "law of Christ" (1 Cor. 9:21)? How can history be seen today as the *topos* ("place") of advent, as a future from a Christian heritage, the coming-upon-us of that which was accomplished in Jesus Christ? How does he still wield his power as the Lord who internally dominates history, not merely as history's transcendental guarantor? Has not the process of secularization long ago put him in the corner, from which only the metaphysical acrobatics of theology can entice him out? How is his "spirit" still poured out over the face of this secular world? How does that which presses upon us with ever greater urgency historically derive its force from the "hour of Christ"? How is the theology of history not merely an elaborate mystique to disguise the godlessness of our present situation?

One could answer, and thereby lay one's finger on a vital point, that the Christian understanding of history stands under the sign of the cross and therefore also under the permanent protest of the world against God. In the process of secularization, the cross proclaims itself an enduring existential principle of the Christian economy of salvation; the secular world in which we find ourselves is in fact nothing other than the expression, lifted onto a cosmic plane, of that worldly opposition to the Holy, to God and his Christ, which is always to be expected in a Christian view of history.[6]

But we must go a step further; we must see in the process of secularization in the world today not only, nor even principally, the necessary negative element in the movement of history as understood by the Christian, but in the last analysis a *positive* Christian value. In other words, the secularization of the world is not unambiguously the world's protesting rejection of God's acceptance of it, but is also and primarily the historical manifestation of its acceptance by God. The secularization of the world must be understood not simply and essentially as the overpowering of Christ in the world through the opposition to him which has heightened with history, but as the most decisive moment of his reign in history.

In this sense let us search more resolutely for the theological basis of this secularization, in order by it to orientate our understanding of the world through faith. In anticipation we can formulate our viewpoint in a thesis which both delimits our area and indicates the position—one mainly of the theology of history—which we shall take up in the wider theme of "a believer's look at the world." The thesis runs roughly: The secularism of the world, as it has come about in the modern process of secularization and as it confronts us today in a universally accentuated form, has come about in its broad lines (though, of course, not in all its historical details) not in spite of *but on account of Christianity*. In origin it is a *Christian* event and thereby witnesses to the historically active power of the "hour of Christ" in our world situation.

II. A CHRISTIAN BASIS FOR UNDERSTANDING THE WORLD

At first sight this thesis may seem strange. Might not one have expected the exact opposite? Does not the power of the Christian spirit to change history appear precisely in the increasing inclusion of the world in the reality of salvation bestowed by Christ, in the final disappearance of the difference between sacred and profane? Is not the world seen to be Christian precisely as the "matter" to be saved, as the starting point of a universal cosmic liturgy? And for this reason, does not the essence of Christendom consist in a continuous struggle against the secularization of the world?

At the moment we must leave these questions unanswered. But we hope that they will find at least an indirect answer if we begin with a direct attempt to provide a positive basis for our thesis. To this end let us very briefly consider the event historically accomplished in Christ which contributes to an understanding of the world. Naturally, even an outline of this event in all its breadth and depth is out of the question; everything we say will be determined by our overriding preoccupation with a theological interpretation of the secular world today.

But, granted this foreshortening, the event which is Christ could be formulated in the following basic statement: *God took the world to himself with final definitiveness in his Son Jesus Christ*. For "the Son of God, Jesus Christ, . . . did not hesitate between Yes and No; the Yes of God has become history [*gegonen*], through him the Amen is made present" (2 Cor. 1:19 f.). And the Church founded by him is the historically visible and effective sign, the sacrament of the eschatologically definitive acceptance of the world by God.

(Of course, the dichotomy of Church and world is the historical manifestation of the world's culpable rejection of its acceptance in the Logos. Indeed, if the world had not protested and opposed its acceptance, there would be no Church either, for the Church is always antagonistically different from the world, being the *ecclesia ex corde scisso*. Therefore, the world itself instead of the Church would unambiguously be the actuality of God's acceptance, and its history would be the unveiled re-presentation of the definitive proximity of God.)

How is this basic statement significant for our purpose? Above all, there is in it a proposition about God and the world which can be distinguished both formally and materially; formally: *God acts on the world in history*; materially: *God's action on the world is such that he takes it irreversibly to himself in his Son.*

1. First, let us deal with the former.

a) What does it formally say to us about God? God, according to this proposition, is a God of history. Our belief in him is not the dramatically clothed externalization of man's timeless metaphysical self-consciousness; it is rather the answer to a historically unique event. For us, God is not merely the changeless, colorless and shapeless horizon of our being, present but nevertheless withdrawn into the infinite distance and inapproachability of his transcendence. He is not the equation of the ground of our being, asymptotic and producible to infinity. He is Emmanuel, the God of a historical moment. His very transcendence has become an event, and is not only the supra-historical "out there," but also the definitive and inescapable future of man which is already present and effective within history.[7]

In this connection we must never forget that God is not some random fact *within* history.⁸ It is not merely that he stands in higher ethico-religious estimation than all other figures in history, and for this reason possesses an exemplary character. But even more so is he of decisive importance for the reality which is history itself. He is lord not only *over* history, insofar as he acts in it (one among other historical events) and sets up a universal kingdom in it (one among other kingdoms), but he is also lord of history in that he constitutes it by giving it its very historical basis (cf. Col. 1:17). For this reason he claims history for himself not merely subsequently, but rather as belonging to him in its origin, insofar as he has made it to be genuine history and insofar as his kingdom in history, the Church, is the sign of this eschatological founding of history.⁹

b) Now let us pursue our inquiry further. What does our basic statement formally affirm about the *world*? Above all, this world in which God acts is no mere world of things and nature but essentially a *world of men* and history; it is a world in which man himself has entered with his understanding and his free action. For this activity of God in the world always raises the question of man, and so of the world as signifying man's existence.¹⁰ This anthropocentrically understood world, through the free, contingent action of God in it, becomes visible as a world of history.¹¹

To conceive of the reality of the world *as the fixed frame within which* occurs the indifferent and finally fatal cycle of the same never-changing history is to think in Greek rather than Christian terms.¹² It would be truer to say that the world comes to be through what happens in it in history; "becoming historical" or, if one prefers, "being made historical" enters into the description of its reality.¹³ *In its very being,* the world is the existential expression of highly diverse, free, contingent origins, and it is just this which conditions the concrete, irreducible multiplicity of its reality: ¹⁴ world-history has diverse "gods" and "lords" (cf. 1 Cor. 8:5).

The definitive, historical action of God *on* the world (not precisely *in* the world) reveals the world ¹⁵ not only as historical in the general sense, but as eschatological; in a process which the world itself can never fully comprehend, it must still gather in the harvest which has already been planted in it. It must seek its own reality in order to become that which through Jesus Christ it already is: the new age, the "new heaven and new earth" (Apoc. 21:1), the single kingdom of God and man.[16]

2. Let us now turn to the content of our basic theological statement and remind ourselves once again that we want to explore it with reference to a theological understanding of our secular world today. Materially, this basic statement tells us: "Through his Son, God so acts on the world that he takes it to himself with eschatological definitiveness." But what does this mean? [17]

a) Our definition will depend on our comprehending this acceptance correctly in the divine dialectic without any Monophysitic misunderstanding—a misunderstanding which has too often and too persistently prevailed in the history of Christendom. In Jesus Christ, man and his world were definitively and irreversibly accepted by the eternal Word: in hypostatic union, as the Church and the theologians say.

So everything which is true of the nature Christ took to himself is basically true of the acceptance by God of man and his world; [18] but this does not mean that everything which is human and worldly is revealed through this acceptance as provisional, a mere sketch, and in the last analysis unreal. Christ's human freedom suffered no loss by being taken up into the divine Word; it was not degraded to the level of a lifeless tool, of a mere stage-player or gesture of God in the world. On the contrary, it was thereby brought to the almost undreamed-of foundation of its being: Jesus Christ was totally man, more human than any of the rest of us.[19]

God does not violate what he takes to himself. He does not suck it up into himself or divinize it in a bad sense of pantheism. God is not like one of the gods; he is not a usurper, not a Moloch. God, precisely because he is God, not only allows the other to remain distinct from himself when he unites the other to himself, but rather constitutes the other precisely as other insofar as he unites it to himself. He can and wants to accept it precisely in the respect in which it differs from himself, in which it is not divine but rather human and worldly.

This capacity constitutes the sole reason for his joy in creating the world and finally in accepting it in his eternal Word. God's acceptance is then in origin more a free gift to that which has its own property and characteristics and independence than a desire to take it to himself. His truth "makes us free" (cf. John 8:32); by his acceptance he sets the object of his gift free for its own authentic mode of being.

It is he—and this is precisely the majesty of his freedom—who grants and guarantees the otherness of the other. He is not the rival of the world; he is its guarantor. The specific importance of the world is increased by the advent of God. The faded pearl sparkles when the rays of his sun incline towards it; he does not extinguish the light of that which is not divine, but makes it shine more authentically according to its origin—in fact to his own greatest glory.[20]

In following this train of thought, we are constantly misled by drawing the formal model for our ontological understanding of God's acceptance of the world more from the realm of nature than from that of existence.[21] But our understanding of what occurs in this acceptance must receive its overriding (formal but not material) orientation from authentically human conditions. Let us compare the relationship which occurs between friends. The deeper a person is accepted and assented to by his friend, all the more does he become himself, all the more does he grow free in his own potentialities. Here acceptance and independence are not opposed, but complement each other and increase proportionately.

Only when it has been accepted does the world become itself in all its deepest worldly potentialities, not although, but precisely because it is taken by God himself into the center of the trinitarian life. Finally, the comparison with human friendship shows us another point: only this liberating acceptance of the world enables it to belong to God in the deepest sense. In the same way, an enfranchised slave, now as a free friend, can belong to his former master more radically and can be taken more basically and all-embracingly into his service.[22]

b) We have said that what God calls to himself he calls to fulfil its own self. But the factor which controls the creature's deepest being is its infinite distance from God. For in his acceptance God remains himself; he continues to be the only reason and basis for the diversity from himself.[23] When he approaches, the distance and difference from him do not disappear ("inconfuse": Denz. 302); on the contrary, only then do they at last become visible.

What he takes to himself comes to him in its creatureliness and so in its nondivinity. *Ipsa assumptione creatur,* says Augustine profoundly of Christ's human nature.[24] In and through its acceptance by the divine Logos, it is given reality as a creature, as something nondivine. It is precisely in God's acceptance of the nondivine that he is differentiated from it as transcendental creator. Through his descent into the world, God is seen in his inexpressible sublimity over the world, in his radical transcendence as creator. Descent and transcendence grow in the same proportion.

By preaching the acceptance of the world in the incarnation of the eternal Word, Christianity at the same time emphasizes the radical uniqueness of God as transcendent creator of the world, as the *Deus semper major,* who "dwells in inaccessible light" (1 Tim. 6:16), and the world as the nondivine work of his hands. For Christianity the understanding of the creatureliness of the world must always be grasped in the understanding of the world through salvation-history.[25] Therefore our understanding of the creatureliness and the finiteness of the world is not lessened but sharpened and intensified when it is understood in terms of the historical reality of salvation.

By the acceptance of the world in Jesus Christ, the world does not become a part of God nor God an internal sector of the universe; nor does this acceptance result in an immediate divinization (*Theiosis*) of this world, but rather only because of this acceptance and precisely in it does the world then appear fully as worldly and God fully as divine. The world becomes visible not somehow in its divinity, but precisely in its nondivinity or its worldliness (how could it be otherwise?), in which God claims it for himself (as the radically other) and over which he rules in his "spirit." One who seriously considers this, who constantly attends to the inner dialectic contained in the event of the acceptance of the world, cannot suspect the world picture here developed of being a "cheap" incarnational optimism which allows the world to be divinized directly through the incarnation or which interprets salvation-history itself as the growing divinization of the world.

To sum up, we can say: Through Jesus Christ, God's infinite "Yes" to the finite world enters history (cf. 2 Cor. 1:19 f.). In this infinite Yes, the finite as such wins a presence and a power which it could never have achieved of itself, since its own Yes to itself can never be more than finite.

Here we end the discussion of our basis for an understanding of the world in faith with respect to secularization today. We should merely add, to avoid a possible misunderstanding, that we have described the acceptance of the world in Jesus Christ primarily in abstract terms, for the sake of a general view; but it must always be conceived as basically and permanently connected with the concrete, historical events of Jesus' life.

The descent into the "flesh of sin" is a *suffering* acceptance, and hence the liberating appropriation of the world, too, is always veiled and characterized by the mark of contradiction. The passion and death of Jesus are built-in, ever-present moments in this acceptance, which may never be thought of as the isolated, purely biological event of his birth. It is, rather, the totality of Christ's life as a person in history, as destiny, which is accomplished and achieved only on the cross.[26]

III. THE SECULARIZATION OF THE WORLD AS THE HISTORICAL RE-PRESENTATION OF THE MYSTERY OF CHRIST

The twofold truth of the Christ-event, as showing forth the world for the first time fully as world and God fully as God in his transcendental superiority to the world, is now effective in the economy of history, which stands under the "law of Christ" (1 Cor. 9:21); it forms a perspective for a genuine Christian understanding of the world. For the world's future remains wholly an inheritance from the hour of Christ (cf. 1 Cor. 10:11, Eph. 1:10, 1 Pet. 4:7).[27]

In its historical progress, the world penetrates ever deeper into its historical origin, provided that it puts itself ever more genuinely under the star and law of its beginning, which consists in being accepted by God in Jesus Christ. Certainly, to the extent that we can neither dispose of nor comprehend within history this origin and this heritage, to this extent the future presaged by this origin remains hidden, too; it remains a future truly beyond our control and our power to alter, being as it is in a world in which the power of the origin entrusted to the world is gradually coming over it as an advent.

From a Christian viewpoint, the world is necessarily related to man, so that it is to be considered as man's understanding of it. A statement about the world from the theology of history is therefore primarily and concretely an anthropological statement about our understanding of it. Hence we can say: The understanding of the world lives—whether one likes this expression or not—from the historical power of the world-perspective projected in Christ, from his spirit, the spirit of Christ (1 Cor. 2:16). This spirit, in fact, reveals nothing new, but draws everything from Christ (cf. Jn. 16:14), so that in this spirit and its activity,[28] the Christ-event is made historically objective and accomplished; it re-presents itself in a basically new world horizon, which could not have been deduced a priori.[29]

In order to assess the astounding significance of the world-view opened up by the Christ-event, we need only look at the world picture in the midst of which the Christian message had to spread and become articulate: that of the Greeks. For the Greeks the world had already experienced the numinous, the dark and obscure beginning of God himself, a twilight of the gods in all its perspectives.

This view did not allow the world to be wholly worldly because it did not allow God to be wholly divine. It is well known that the Greek world picture lacked the conception of a transcendent Creator-God. God was thought of more as a principle of the world, a law or reason behind the universe, as regulating it from within. The divine itself was an element in the Greek picture of the world.[30] But this immediate glow of divinity in the world, this mystico-religious veiling—the apotheosis of nature and the piety of the world based on it—is unchristian, genuinely pagan. Only the pagans, says Paul, know "many gods and lords of the world but we have only the one God from whom all comes and to whom we tend" (1 Cor. 8:5 f.), the transcendent God, who is not to be found in the perspective of the world itself, but allows the world to be worldly.

For this reason Christianity, precisely because the consideration of her origin led her to an ever deeper awareness of her nature, inevitably appeared not as increasing divinization, but as a mounting removal of divinity from the world; in this sense it was seen as a profanation of the world, removing from it magic and myth. So it is no mere chance that the pagans, caught up in a Greek world-view, branded the Christians, with an uncanny flair for the truth, as the real and pernicious *a-theoi*, the atheists who delivered the world to god-lessness.[31]

It cannot be denied that this antique world picture held sway in the history of western Christendom for many a year. Even of the high Middle Ages we must today say that its world picture was in general strangely antique, dominated by an immediate "divinism" (Y. Congar). And we should like to think that it is only because deep down we make this unrefined medieval world picture the guiding light of our Christian view of the world, that the modern secularization of the world causes us any embarrassment.

In fact, however, behind this modern process of the increasing secularization of the world there also lies a genuinely Christian impulse. We need only judge this universal process of secularization, and the cosmic atheism which is taking control of it, in the light of the Christological principle developed above to see that this process is in its basic trait (admittedly *only* in this) directed not against a Christian world-view, but rather against an immediate cosmic divinism. Indeed, this process appears to represent exactly what has occurred in our world situation through the Christ-event.[32]

It is in God's acceptance of the world in Jesus Christ, we said, that occurs the radical and basic liberation of the world for its own character and properties, for the undisguised reality of its non-divinity. This process is historically at work in the modern secularization of the world; here the world appears for the first time as the universal expression of its constitution in the incarnation: that is, as world.

The history of this process has many layers and is far from easy to follow step by step. It is not free from culpable error and the false paths of a hybrid secularism. As new heights of our understanding of the world come into view, the abysses of possible error and lapse become deeper, and the danger of toppling over into them greater. The cautions and protests of the Church against these new ways of the world that tend toward secularization must be assessed primarily against the background of these *concrete* dangers and errors. But our concern here is with the broad line of this tendency as such. If we understand it in the light of our principle, then it is not to be simply and in all respects rejected as a vicious secularism, as the expression of the emancipation of the world in protest against God's definitive advances and their eschatological embodiment, the Church. It must rather be assessed as a sign of the liberation and the establishment of the world in its secularism under God's guidance, though we by no means should or would mean by this that the modern process of secularization and the world-view realized in it are the perfectly adequate expression of the secularization commanded and intended by the Christ-event.

1. Therefore we can understand in a positive way the process begun in the late Middle Ages by which *Imperium* and *Sacerdotium* were separated from each other, and therewith the world and its institutions (notably the State) separated from and made independent of the Church. The State appears now no more as the sacral institution it seemed to be in former days, but as a secular creation of God. It is stripped of its immediate and "unquestionable" numinous and sacral character by a Christianity which proclaims itself responsible for all man's religious connections; it is set free as the original agent of the secular world, and therefore as true partner of the Church.

2. The same can be said of the process by which the secular sciences gained their independence from the universal theological order of knowledge in the Middle Ages, chiefly by way of the growing independence of philosophy. Basically, this is not in opposition to, but rather in accordance with, the spirit of Christianity, whose truth "makes us free" (cf. Jn. 8:32).[33]

The independence of secular reason begins to be visible even in

Thomas Aquinas, insofar as "the philosopher" (Aristotle) appears as an authority on his own account. And after a long path, not easy to follow in the history of philosophy and theology, this process by which human reason became independent finds its official recognition by the Church in Vatican Council I. In the history of modern philosophy, this path has not been trodden without considerable error and has often been misunderstood as the rationalistic emancipation of human reason.

But here we should like only to repeat that once again in this process, a secularization of philosophy, guided and historically necessitated by the Christian spirit itself, is afoot—not because Christianity fideistically neglects philosophy, but precisely because Christianity wants to make full use of it and can do this only insofar as it makes it free in its inner being. In this sense philosophical reasoning has achieved a high and unprecedented degree of independence in modern times, precisely in contrast to the classical Greek philosophy, which never succeeded in critically shaking itself free of its theological origin. Thus the split between sacred and profane wisdom in recent centuries is seen to consist basically, admittedly not in every detail, in their mutual confrontation in free dialogue, as conditioned and occasioned by Christianity.

3. Finally, a third point of view: In modern times, we are seeing nature as an object for human endeavor; we are demythologizing "mother earth" and removing her taboos, an advance which makes her an object of man in his experiments. This process in which nature appears more and more as an object of human activity and therefore becomes more and more secularized is made possible by a deeply Christian impulse; it is in the last analysis an expression of that very secularization of the world which is rooted in the Christ-event. Where this mystery is historically at work in our understanding of the world, nature can appear under her true colors: not as God, but as nature created by God, let loose among its own

laws (secondary causes), which lie open to man's methodical investigation, without the majesty of its creator being thereby impugned.

Christianity has also spontaneously made possible (and certainly not *only* this) the purposeful material investigation of nature. Hence it has really been the first to set in motion that adventure of the modern mind by which nature becomes an "achievement," in which man has a total grasp of the world, and by which the world appears as the material and work *of his own hands*. In this way, everything present within the horizon of the world is seen more and more under the total perspective of man, acknowledging its immediate dependence on him.[34] The world is met as the world of man; we are confronted first and most immediately not by the *vestigia Dei* but by the *vestigia hominis*. God's creation comes to us always through man's achievement and is strongly "anthropocentrically" inclined. Basically, this is all a Christian event.

Of course, this advance, called "technique" in its perfection, has other aspects: it involves the unpredictable atrophy of other fundamental human possibilities; certainly the tendency to materialize remains a very real danger; at the same time it tends to turn against man, attempting to make him the object of its technical preoccupation and its reconstruction.[35] But all the same, in finding our bearings in such an unpersonalized nature, we should bear in mind that it is Christianity which made this situation possible, and we should make this the basis of the position we adopt and the basis of our attempt to deal with the secularized world.

We have been able to make only a few suggestions, and even those in the crudest, almost irresponsibly abbreviated form. Above all, two aspects should be clear: First, that Christianity of its nature effects a sort of secularization of the world; that wherever it becomes historically effective while remaining true to its origins, it appears as a movement to do away with the magic of nature—a secularization of the world, and therefore a demythologizing of the world-view of classical antiquity, which too long and too profoundly remained the effective guiding light of the Christian attitude towards the world. Second, for this reason a true Christian impulse is at work in the modern process of secularization; hence the historical power of the Christian spirit reveals itself once again in this process, and this process itself is therefore by no means the unambiguous expression of the impotence or mere indifference of Christianity to the modern world. What has been happening today in an ever increasing way does not spring from the disappearance of the faith from the world due to the superior power of the world hostile to the faith, but from the historical power of the Christian faith itself, accepting the world and setting it free.

The tragedy of the Christian faith is not the secularization of the world, but rather—or so it seems to us—the way in which we Christians in fact reacted to it, and for the most part still do. Have we not here failed to recognize, or have we even rejected, our own child, so that it ran away in youth and now, totally estranged from us, regards us with a gaze distorted by a vicious secularism? Did not Christianity, at the dawn of modern times, enter too hesitatingly into this new world-perspective?

Have we not shut ourselves off far too much from it, in general thoroughly suspected and despised it, so that we allow the world to "be itself" only with a bad conscience, although the acceptance by God's Word has liberated it into its radical secularism? Do not the inner uncertainty and unsureness of the secular world, its lack of real genuineness, and its false desire for autonomy have such menacing consequences *also* (though of course not only) because Christianity gave the world its freedom hesitatingly and only under protest?

Today one may, indeed must, hazard the assertion that the secularization of the world, in origin a Christian event, was compelled to force itself through in opposition to the concrete historical world-view of Christendom, and that this is the reason why in fact it took on an anti-Christian, viciously secular character.[36] It is just this which makes the historical phenomenon of the modern process of secularization so complicated and almost incomprehensible. Be that as it may, we firmly maintain that basically the process was forwarded and made inevitable by the historical force of the Christ-event, and that insofar as this is true we must still in many fields assimilate it into our Christian consciousness.

But meanwhile, has not the end of the modern age come upon us, as is often proclaimed today? We must answer no in the sense of a theology of history; at least we cannot recognize this end. On the contrary, we should like to think that the modern age, in everything which confronts us, ominous with undelimited, impenetrable profaneness, is only just beginning to dawn, that the full weight of this modern process is only now becoming fully visible, and that it is therefore so much more vital for us to remember that it has become effective in the West through the impulse of Christianity.

It is not to be denied, and can no longer be overlooked, that, just as God's definitive acceptance of the world remains hidden in the cross of his Son, so also its universal historical actualization in the modern process of secularization will never be wholly under our control, never wholly comprehensible to us within the world or within history. The modern secular world will always appear to be contradicting and protesting, shutting itself off from its origin in a vicious secularism; the more accentuated this process grows in history, the more we shall suffer from it, the deeper we shall penetrate into the night of the cross.

We neither can nor may simply identify the modern and actual process of secularization with the secularism which Christ intended and made possible for the world. This would be a mistaken attempt to comprehend univocally and adequately the universal process of salvation-history. When we nevertheless attempted to reach a positive Christian understanding of secularism, we meant it mainly in a *historical sense,* to distinguish and oppose that divinizing world-view which was historically operative until the Middle Ages, and which has receded in modern times. We may never lose sight of the relative nature of our estimate of the specifically modern process of secularization without falling victim to a false identification.

Before we turn briefly to the question of Christian existence in this secular world, we shall sum up again, holding fast to the three points of our world-view which have become visible in our investigations: (1) secularism as not yet historically met by Christianity, and in this sense "inculpable" (as it was in ancient paganism); (2) secularism as set free by the historical dynamism of Christianity; (3) secularism as misunderstanding the liberation process in an autonomous and vicious way, protesting against its Christian origin and emancipating itself from it.[37]

IV. CHRISTIAN EXISTENCE IN A SECULAR WORLD

The liberation of the world into its secularism through the Christ-event leads not to the void of pure desertion of God, but to a deeper way of belonging to him. As mediator and, at the same time, as negotiator of this reversal of the world now liberated for its original responsiveness to God, appears man. More clearly than ever is his responsibility as a Christian obvious. But how should he understand and accomplish it in the perspective of the secularism of the world? By what criterion should he orientate himself?

Basically our reply runs: His relation to the world *is the re-enactment in faith of the descent of God into the world, of the liberating acceptance of the world in Jesus Christ.* The believer's relation to the world is, then, not a matter of deducing the difference from the world, but of determining it by re-enacting in faith

God's action of preserving the world in its secularism. What do we mean by this?

The believer today finds himself in a world made up of the most diverse and contradictory tendencies and inclinations. As a believer, he has entered into the world as such—through his profession and circumstances of life—without integrating his attitude to the world wholly into his faith. He finds he is acting upon the world in a way which is not primarily determined or given its theme by his faith. This pluralism in the guiding principles of life is, it seems to us, unavoidable today; it has been remarked upon in various ways.[38] Thus the believer easily gets the impression that his existence has a double foundation, that he lives from a double standard of truth, that his existence is an ellipse rather than a circle, centered on two poles, between which the march of his being rotates. For the relation between the two factors, faith and the world, can no longer be comprehended and fixed by faith itself. Abandonment to the world is not even thematically convertible with abandonment to God; it remains firmly stuck in the pure secularism of the world.

The course of the believer's life today is, therefore, basically and in all its details determined by a permanent and (unless we are mistaken) permanently broadening dichotomy. Nor can one simply leave this dichotomy unresolved. For in the long run, it would be wholly obscured by the overpowering world. But if we take the secularism of the world seriously—as a Christian should—this dichotomy cannot be completely resolved by simply bringing the world expressly into the sphere of faith, by making it the theme of an act of faith. As Christians, we must ever more and more take to ourselves in the re-enactment of the *descensus Christi* those elements of the world which are not yet assimilated into our faith, for it is from the world and for the world that we live; this is precisely how we set the world free in faith, how we leave to it its own worldly character.

For example, a young man wants to become an engineer. This is a project for life, a form of decisive entry into the world which may precede the decision of faith, may precede his personal acceptance of God's love, or at least not proceed from it. The young man should get to the point where his faith overtakes his decision; [39] his profession as engineer, which cannot and does not want to be anything but a firm partnership with the world, should be assimilated by his faith, and so be more basically occasioned by it.

The irresoluble dichotomy which reigns in him should be seen to originate in, and be resolved by, his faith. The worldly character of his existence as an engineer should be safeguarded by the freedom and discretion of his faith: "All things are for you, whether it be Paul, or Apollo, or Cephas; or the world, or life, or death; or things present, or things to come; it is all for you—and you for Christ and Christ for God" (1 Cor. 3:22 f.). What is worldly in the world can be integrated in a genuine Christian way, and the believer has no immediate reason to have a bad conscience in entering into it.

Of course, there is one factor which cannot be overlooked without dangerously abbreviating and misrepresenting the event of secularism: we ourselves can never assimilate the world in such a way that its secularism appears as the *pure* expression of our acceptance, of its liberation through our faith. For the origin of this liberating acceptance of the world is not in ourselves. Its origin is nothing other than the *descensus* of the Son, in whom the Father has definitively taken the world to himself. Because we do not accomplish this acceptance, but only re-enact it in the grace of Jesus Christ, the secularism of the world never appears to us as receiving its equilibrium and its freedom from our acceptance of it in faith. The situation of the world in faith remains always diastatic. Secularism always appears as something beyond our control, not penetrated by faith itself, and, in this sense, really pagan and profane.[40]

Indeed, the world is wholly within the grasp of Christianity, not in us and in our historical situation in faith, but in God and his acceptance of the world. He alone, in the inscrutable mystery of his love, is the only genuine meeting place between faith and the world. For he alone originally set the difference between the two by the incarnation; and only in its origin is it also overcome, not in the leveling one-sidedness of a vicious pantheism, but in the God who is all in all (1 Cor. 15:28), in which both are united in inviolable independence.

But for us this unity within the world and within history remains beyond our grasp. For us the visible acceptance of the world in its secularism remains an eschatological event, in the hope of which we live. At present, the phenomenon of this secularism remains on many different levels and can never be undialectically reduced to one denominator; it keeps its own inherent and irresoluble multivalence. Our relation to it as Christians is truly neither unprejudiced nor unquestioningly optimistic. It cannot at all be described in clear categories, for it cannot be rigidly defined or comprehended; it "changes" as a variable function.[41]

The re-enactment in faith of the liberating acceptance of the world remains for us painfully hidden in an almost impenetrable and obscure secularism. We shall always have to suffer from this secularism and bear it as the cross of our faith, appearing as it does extremely pagan and profane. We shall always have to confess with Paul: "I am crucified to the world and the world to me" (Gal. 6:14). This is so not in spite of our acceptance of its secularism, but precisely *because* we accept it in faith, and because it is for us painfully strange and ever estranging in this incomprehensible state, gloomy and as though sightless, in the very center of the realization of our faith.[42]

We terminate with a question: Can it nevertheless be evident, in our attitude to this world as believers, that the world has been definitively accepted in all its secularism? How is it shown that our faith is a specifically Christian faith that knows that the world has already been taken to himself by God, indeed, that knows that the world can become visible in its radical secularism only insofar as it already lies within the grasp of God's liberating acceptance? By this we mean that our faith, and basically *our faith alone*, can boldly stand up to its worldliness, and take it to itself as it is.[43]

This peaceful and respectful insertion of ourselves into the secularism of the world is really in itself an unthematic (so to speak, "transcendental") religious act, which has its place concretely in the perspective of the Christ-event. For only from this viewpoint can such a secularism be borne without itself being once again remolded, sublimated, or given a vicious secular embellishment and a veiled cult of profaneness. When all is said and done, only a Christian can take secularism really seriously, in itself, without undermining or overwhelming it with an ideology and so dulling the edge of its material profaneness.[44]

This does not mean that the Christian experiences the world in a purely "make-believe" sort of way, and only the unbeliever as it really is. On the contrary, through the Christ-event the world has achieved so radical a form of its secularism, has become so god-less through God's liberating acceptance, that only on the strength of this event can man today stand up to it without giving his allegiance to new gods.[45]

The unbelieving non-Christian will always be led to a false ideology by this accentuated secularism, either to the utopia of a naive belief in progress, in a worldly paradise, or to a tragic nihilism and resigned skepticism. This is how new forms of mythology come into existence in the midst of our secular world. And, like all myths, they have something violent and fabricated, but at the same time restrictive, about themselves. It is these unbelieving non-Christians, and not really the secularism of the world, who are the bane of our time, who constitute the real danger to the believer.

In contrast to them, it is the Christian who appears as the really "worldly" man, for only he can truly tolerate what is worldly, relying upon his re-enactment in faith of that act which gives everything worldly in the world its being and its life: God's liberating acceptance of the world in Jesus Christ. But this tolerance is no mere passivity or indifference to the world; it is the highest completion of the world in the spirit and power of that freedom into which we have been introduced by Christ, and to which we are ever called anew.[46] "The victory which has overcome the world is our faith, for no one overcomes the world but he who believes that Jesus is the Son of God" (1 Jn. 5:4–6). Faith overcomes the world; this means that it sets man basically free from the world. But in this freedom, the believer walks by the side of the Son of God in his acceptance of the world; in the strength of the Son of God, he too can truly take the world to himself, preserve the world, tolerate it, and precisely in its worldliness make it the visible expression of the love of God in Jesus Christ.[47]

"To Christianize the world"—such has always been considered the task of the Christian in the world. It can be understood in a correct and vitally decisive sense; but to us it seems a very misleading expression. For "Christianize" may not, in view of everything we have said, be used to mean "make different" from what it is: world; it may not be used to mean to cover or remold the world with something unworldly or supra-worldly, to plant a new dimension on top of it, or—as people love to say—to "bring it home" from its secularism into a numinously glowing divinity.

In the same sense must we understand expressions like "Christian art," "Christian philosophy," "Christian State," and so forth. There is no question here of a "Christianization" in the sense of an additional remolding or sublimation of these realities; it is a matter of their insertion into their origin and their true properties (art, philosophy, State, as such). The adjective "Christian," if rightly understood, is therefore not an alienating addition, but rather an intensification of the worldly reality which *concretely* (because of God's saving intervention in history) contains deeper dimensions and more basic properties than it can realize from its own nature.

We can say, therefore, that to Christianize the world means in its basic sense to make the world more worldly, to bring it into its own, to preserve the barely suggested, barely dreamed-of heights and depths of its own worldly nature which have been made possible by grace, but have been hidden and obstructed by sin. For it is sin which estranges the world from itself. Sin has real power, and grants to the world something which is not its own nature. Sin (and in sin the "Father of Sin") does not preserve or let be. Sin is itself not freedom but slavery, and enslaves everything; it remolds, embellishes, conceals the nature of things.

But grace is freedom, preserving things in the almost unsounded depths of their being. In its saving power, grace calls and guides them from their sinful estrangement into their own. It calls and guides the world into its perfect secularism. *Gratia perficit naturam* is true also of the consecration of the world through grace; grace seals the world in its deepest secularism, leads the world in an incomparable way into its own home, gives it its own in an undreamed-of manner.

And the Church, the historical visible sign and institution of this grace in the world, is therefore not the opponent but the guarantor of the world. The Church exists indeed for the sake of the world. For the world is—to transform a well-known saying—the end of God's road. The Church herself is in the service of God's universal will for the world.[48] She attests and makes present the rule of that incarnate will in which God definitively claims the world for himself and, by so doing, grants the world its freedom to be itself.

Certainly it is not for us within history to build up the full secularism of the world, to bring the world into its own. This remains an eschatological act of God in which he will consummate for the world what has already happened to it by the universal historical recapitulation in Jesus Christ. But it is clear from everything we have said that this world which is eschatologically consummated is by no means sucked up by God or divinized in a bad sense; rather, it is a world for which God is "all in all," because he has set it free into its own and into its highest independence through his infinite love and because he generously guarantees its freedom. What the basic and autonomous entity of the world is—what the nature of its secularism in the fullest sense consists of—is a question which can be answered only eschatologically, through the whole of the as yet incomplete history of the world.

At this point we must close. We have been concerned all along to show and attest the secularism of the world in a Christian perspective, to show that this, too, or rather *precisely this* stands under the law of the Hour of Christ and his grace. We have tried to show that its future, although it presses upon us in all its incomprehensible obscurity, has its roots in the historical power of the Son of Man—less obviously perhaps, less in the foreground and so more discreetly, but all the same present in an indomitability which is without precedent.

NOTES

[1] Cf. J. B. Metz, "Die Zukunft des Glaubens in einer hominisierten Welt," in: *Hochland* 56 (1964), pp. 377–91. In this essay the author develops the anthropological aspects of this secularization and investigates the concrete possibility of the Christian faith in such a secularized world.

[2] Cf. K. Rahner, "Christianity and the 'New Man'" in this book.

[3] Cf. G. Thils, *Theologie der irdischen Wirklichkeiten*, Salzburg o. J.

[4] Cf. the well-known work of A. Auer, *Weltoffener Christ, Grundsätzliches und Geschichtliches zur Laienfrömmigkeit* (2nd ed.; Düsseldorf: 1962).

[5] Cf.—despite the stress on openness—A. Auer, *ibid.*, pp. 59 ff.

[6] For an attempt to give an interpretation of our world situation from

the theology of history, cf. J. B. Metz, "Die 'Stunde' Christi," in: *Wort und Wahrheit* 12 (1957), pp. 5–18.

[7] We cannot treat here for itself the question, so important for a theology of history, why the trinitarian God acts on us precisely in his eternal Word. Cf. K. Rahner, *Schriften zur Theologie III* (Einsiedeln: 1956), pp. 40–46; *IV* (Einsiedeln: 1960), pp. 96 f., 118–120, 137 ff. (Eng. tr.: *Theological Investigations III and IV* [Baltimore: Helicon, 1964, 1965].)

[8] Cf. J. B. Metz, *op. cit.*, pp. 5 f.

[9] To understand the power of Jesus Christ in history, it is essential to consider this *inner (transcendental) difference* in the phenomenon of history itself. The incarnation is not a "principle" which one applies afterwards to certain phenomena in history, but is the internal *principium* of history itself, its "starting point" (Col. 1:17), its "basis" (Apoc. 3:14), its progressive and all-embracing goal, its "A" and "O" (Apoc. 1:18), its "fullness" (Gal. 4:4; Mark 1:15), its concrete realization, in which time's before and after become true history. It is only when the controlling basis of history is thought of historically that its historical character becomes fully evident.

[10] "World" should not be understood exclusively cosmocentrically and objectivistically; it must also be thought of anthropocentrically, as man's relation to and understanding of it.

[11] Only from an anthropocentric point of view can the world be understood historically. God can act on the world truly historically only insofar as it is the world of men.

[12] Cf. R. Bultmann, *Das Verständnis von Welt und Mensch im NT und im Griechentum: Glaube u. Verstehen II* (Tübingen: 1952), pp. 59–78.

[13] It is not a statistical measure, not primarily a condition, but more basically a happening. History is not added on to an already constituted nature of the world, but rather belongs to the ontological constitution of the world itself. Therefore the world is in its very constitution more than can be said about it through metaphysical reflection.

[14] We can say this in theological terms: existentially it is already formed in advance by the action of Adam (or even more basically by the culpable action of the angels, which is not wholly cut off from the world), and by the saving action of Christ with respect to the world.

[15] "Reveal" has here an ontological sense: being revealed means coming forward and rising to the actuality of a thing's own historical reality.

[16] Here is also to be seen a formal, historical world-conception, which can be assessed and revised in the light of faith; for example, the monistic conception of dialectical materialism. For also, and precisely, for a historical understanding of the world by Christians, transcendence is not totally outside the world, but something which genuinely lasts and stands out in history—only that this unity of God and the world in the medium of history is controlled not by us, but by God himself (who alone can maintain the difference from us in the unity which he freely communicates to us).

[17] Let us here indicate a point of view not considered expressly enough in the text: the definitive acceptance of the world by God in Jesus Christ implies also that the "prince of this world" is already "cast out" (cf. Jn. 12:31; 16:11; Lk. 10:18; Col. 2:15; and other passages). His "power" may neither be gnostically absolutized in an apotheosis of evil, nor be leveled down to a merely transitory, comprehensible and escapable action. It is more an existential remolding (starting from a historical origin), a universal negative invasion of our concrete historical sphere of freedom. Seen in the light of a theology of history, it is already diminishing. It is by no means on the same level as the saving action of God in Jesus Christ, which is not merely accomplished within an all-embracing history (one among other historical powers), but which has itself given history its historical character.

[18] We consider here—for the sake of the conciseness required—the assumed nature of Christ as an expression of God's basic acceptance of man and his world. If one conceives this assumption of Christ's human nature rightly and follows it to its logical conclusion that the divine Logos remains forever man and a man of this world, one cannot deny our extrapolation of the Christological principle to the basic reality of the God-World relationship. In his spirit, in which the incarnate Word remains with us, this permanent and irreversible acceptance of man's world is guaranteed to us—without making any difference in the formal predetermination of the individual's salvation.

[19] Consider also his gift of integrity, through which he was not preserved from the abyss of human suffering and uncertainty, but suffered it to the end more radically, continuously, and uncompromisingly than we men who have concupiscence.

[20] So also the true greatness and freedom of a man are to be seen in his tolerance of others, not allowing them to pale, shrivel or disappear beside himself, but bringing them to their own original, almost undreamed-of brilliance in his presence for the first time, letting them find themselves.

[21] For the task of thinking of the reality of revelation primarily in existential ("anthropocentric") and not natural ("cosmocentric") categories, cf. J. B. Metz, *Christliche Anthropozentric, zur Denkform des Thomas von Aquin* (Munich: 1962), pp. 108–15. (An English translation will soon be published: New York.)

[22] The relations here laid down are ontological, not merely moral, as could be the case in an ontology primarily oriented by the material data; cf. J. B. Metz, *ibid.*, p. 87.

[23] Cf. K. Rahner, "Current Problems in Christology," in: *Theological Investigations I* (Baltimore: Helicon, 1961), pp. 180–85.

[24] St. Augustine, *Contra sermonem Arianorum* 8,6 (PL 42, 688). For the Christological significance of this axiom, cf. F. Malmberg, *Über den Gottmenschen* (Freiburg: 1960), pp. 38 ff.

[25] In the New Testament we primarily meet God not as the transcendental creator of the world, and the world not in its creaturely dependence on him, but God as the Father of our Lord Jesus Christ, and the world as touched by him in the history of salvation. The theological understanding of creation and creatureliness (or finiteness) must always be seen in the perspective of salvation-history. In this connection we may mention the doctrine, wholly acceptable to Catholics, that the reason why God did not allow the fallen order of nature wholly to estrange itself from him was that the sin which disturbed this order remained always contained within his progressive will to save in Jesus Christ; thus in the last resort the whole state of nature and creation since the fall is seen theologically to be the expression of God's will in salvation-history to save; cf. H. Küng, "Christozentrik," in: *LThK II*, pp. 1169–74. Cf. also H. Küng, *Justification* (Westminster: 1964).

[26] For this continuous and total unity of the event of the incarnation, for the passion as an internal element of the incarnation, cf. J. B. Metz, "Armut in Geiste, vom Geist der Menschwerdung Gottes und der Menschwerdung des Menschen," in: *Geist und Leben* 34 (1961), pp. 419–35.

[27] Cf. J. B. Metz, "Die 'Stunde' Christi," pp. 9–14.

[28] This "spirit of Christ" is the true "objective spirit" of history, which is not, of course, penetrated merely intellectually, but can be received only in a genuine historical decision ("faith").

[29] We cannot further develop the specific sequence of cause and effect which we presuppose as holding sway in history. The cause (itself a historical occurrence) causes by going out to meet and representing itself (in both senses of the word) historically in that which is to be caused.

[30] It must be said that even the radical rejection of the world in late hellenistic Gnosticism is really another instance of religious mystification and not a pure secularization of the world; cf. H. Jonas, *Gnosis und spätantiker Geist I* (Göttingen: 1954), p. 150 (Eng. tr.: *The Gnostic Religion: The Message of the Alien God and the Beginning of Christianity* [1964]); F. Gogarten, *Verhängnis und Hoffnung der Neuzeit* (2nd ed.; Stuttgart: 1958), p. 23.

[31] It would be possible to show that in the Christological heresies of the early Church there was an unchristian world picture at work.

[32] F. Gogarten reaches a new assessment similar to ours of the modern process of secularization in his important book *Hoffnung der Neuzeit* —admittedly starting from a totally different theological perspective. (Cf. note 28.)

[33] Cf. J. B. Metz, "Theologische und Metaphysische Ordnung," in: *ZkTh* 83 (1961), especially pp. 10–14. We have taken some sentences word for word.

[34] Cf. U. v. Balthasar, *Die Gottesfrage des heutigen Menschen* (Vienna-Munich: 1956), pp. 26 ff.

[35] On this subject cf. K. Rahner, "Christianity and the 'New Man.'" (Cf. note 2.)

[36] A parallel is to be found in the relationship of "Christian philosophy" and modern thought; cf. J. B. Metz, *Christliche Anthropozentrik*, p. 128. (Cf. note 21.)

[37] A parallel is the triple relationship of philosophy to Christianity: J. B. Metz, *ibid.*, p. 131. (Cf. also note 21.)

[38] Cf. K. Rahner, "The Order of Redemption within the Order of Creation," in: *The Christian Commitment* (New York: 1963), pp.

38–74, esp. 69 ff.; U. v. Balthasar, *Schleifung der Bastionen* (Einsiedeln: 1952).

[39] For there is nothing in my worldly existence which could not appear to be sent by God's love, though, of course, there is nothing in a worldly world which unequivocally must be the result of this love.

[40] In theological language we could also say that our concrete world-view remains "concupiscent," that is, remains unable to assimilate the worldliness of the world as an expression of its liberating acceptance in faith.

[41] For the New Testament, "change" is a basic characteristic of the believer's world-view; cf. U. v. Balthasar, *op. cit.*, p. 63. (Cf. also note 36.)

[42] Here is also revealed a characteristic of the world as it in fact is: the world has no desire to remain just itself. It is the world, not faith, which is a Moloch, wanting to suck everything up into itself; this is just why it opposes a faith which removes its magic, strips off this mythological claim and puts it on its own; the world protests and cuts itself off.

[43] Cf. K. Rahner, *op. cit.* (Cf. also note 36.)

[44] So it is by no means the task of the Christian to draw the profane ever more fully into the sacred and sanctify it in this *immediate* sense; rather it is to set it free again and again from the sacred and in this *mediate* sense to sanctify it.

[45] This is so true that one is compelled to say that, whenever a non-Christian sincerely stands up against this worldliness, he does it by virtue of a hidden Christianity.

[46] This freedom given to the world by Christ is used especially by F. Gogarten as a starting point of his interpretation of the modern process of secularization. (Cf. note 30.)

[47] This tolerant acceptance of the world, this positive guaranteeing is the basic act of Christian asceticism with respect to the world. Indeed, Christian asceticism basically subserves this acceptance; it is not really a thorough rejection, which in the last analysis is much easier to carry out than the acceptance; cf. J. B. Metz, "Armut im Geiste." (Cf. note 24.)

[48] The Church must be understood within the framework of God's universal will for the world: God wills the world, and not really the

Church as opposed to the world. The Church as opposed to the world came into being only because God's living acceptance of the world was rejected with protests by the world. The Church is the sign and guarantee of God's final victory over a world which contradicts and culpably deteriorates, and for this reason is untrue to itself. Hence we must always regard the Church as that embarrassment (*sit venia verbo!*) which she really is in salvation-history (and for which the world is, in the last analysis, to blame).

PART TWO

The Christian Experiences Christ in the World

The Dominion of Christ

by Heinrich Schlier

THE FOLLOWING REFLECTIONS are not meant to be a treatise in biblical theology on the dominion of Christ; there is not enough space at our disposal for this. Nor are they intended to be an exegesis only for experts. Our purpose is rather a spiritual one. These considerations propose to extend the biblico-theological treatise and to bring the reader a little closer to the matter at hand. One who knows how estranged the seemingly well-known and self-evident content of faith is from today's mentality will not think such an endeavor superfluous.

I

The dominion of Christ over the Church and the world, according to St. Paul, has its foundation in the will of God. This will of God wants "to re-establish all things under one head in Christ" (Eph. 1:9 ff.). The dominion of Christ is not derived from human plans and desires; it is not the result of the work of historical or natural powers. It has its foundation in something beyond all that is in the heavens and on earth, for it has its foundation in God. Because God wants once again to place the universe under one head, and so, in the true sense of the word, to recapitulate all things for himself, there is the dominion of Christ.

God has from all time established the world in Christ as its head. He has also previously fixed the aeons, the epochs of cosmic history in Christ; he has foreseen and foredetermined them for Christ. As the world comes forth out of the eternal will of God, it is borne by this his eternal "good will" in Christ. The world's being is this: to be destined for Christ from time immemorial.

This foresight and foredetermination of the world are, if we may so say, properly inserted by God into creation from the very beginning with the following implications: Since creation is indebted to God, it is indebted to Christ; since it subsists in God, it subsists in Christ; and finally, since it is ordered to God, it is ordered to Christ. One often forgets what Colossians 1:16 ff. says about Christ: "For in him were created all things in the heavens and on the earth. . . . All things have been created through and unto him, and he is before all creatures, and in him all things hold together." (Cf. also 1 Cor. 8:6.)

Christ, according to Ephesians 3, is truly the mystery of the wisdom of God which already ruled hidden in the creator. Everything that exists is not only from the very beginning predestined by God in Christ, but is also directed toward Christ in creation itself. Creation is impregnated with Christ as its foundation and its goal. The dominion of Christ—and this is what has led us to speak of these things—is nothing strange and a priori inimical to the original creation. Quite the opposite: all that is originates in the dominion of Christ.

The dominion of Christ is prepared in creation in such a way that creation is made ready for this dominion. How could this be otherwise, since, according to St. Paul, not only "we who have the Spirit," but also creation itself, subjugated by Adam to vanity, "groans and travails in pain until now" and "with ardent longing awaits" the revelation of the dominion of Christ (Rom. 8:19 ff.)? If this is true, then the dominion of Christ not only will make use of what it has preserved from creation, but will also again set the created universe free, either provisionally or definitively.

II

But the "universe," that totality of "powers," world and man, according to St. Paul, no longer exists as it was first created. The "powers and forces" of the original creation of God have soared up and made themselves and their worldly spheres autonomous. In the foregoing disobedience of Adam, man turns away from God his creator and from himself as a creature; he becomes a renegade from God and from himself. Man thereby not only alienates himself and his world from God in Christ, but also injures his own existence together with his world. Paul does not go any further into the background of this twofold 'fall' of the powers and of men. He sees only the fallen world and interests himself in its present reality. Is not this indeed the world in which we live and in which Christ is going to erect his dominion? Let us therefore call to mind the main characteristics of this our historical world.

It is a world closed up in itself—not closed up on the part of God the creator who continues to call forth life in it, but rather consistently closed up on the part of men and the powers. It is a world dominated by the spirit of autonomy. The domain where this spirit dwells and rules is the "air," that is, the vast and intensive atmosphere in which men at any given moment find their world and their age—the atmosphere in which men live and according to which they understand themselves and their world. Through the atmosphere it has prepared, this ruling spirit of autonomy, this power in opposition to God, presents the world to man as the eternal aeon, as the unique foundation and horizon of his existence.

This spirit causes the world to become that menacing and tempting powerful reality after which man patterns his life. The spirit of autonomy, bestowing always a fascination to the world, captivates the men who breathe its air. In spite of all this, of course, this spirit would still be powerless were it not for that corresponding tendency of man, such as he is since Adam, to greet this offer of an autonomous world. This tendency is what St. Paul calls the "craving of the flesh," in short, the egoistic striving of man toward himself and toward an autonomous world, a striving that dominates his senses and his spirit.

Should man succumb to this fundamental egoism—and this happens continually, for the attachment to self is too great—he then falls into corruption. But he falls into corruption precisely because he yields to pressure from an autonomous and overpowering world, which has been presented to him by the universal spirit of autonomy. In sin, whose process is here described, there is always a twofold reality: I hand myself over to *myself*, and I hand myself over to the *world*, the world which in its autonomy offers itself to me. By injustice and self-justification I thus reinforce the spirit of the autonomous world; both constitute the sin. The threatening and seducing appearance of the autonomous world thus drags me ever deeper into sin.

In such a collaboration of powers and men which makes up human history, their fall culminates in death. For this egoistic turning to myself and to an autonomous world is at the same time a turning away from God and his gift. Now the very act of this turning away is death, for life subsists only in an existence which, turned toward its creator, receives its life from his hands. Life subsists only in the act of reception, as a gift and gratuity.

Since Adam, of course, man does not see through all this. For the turning away from God his creator, or the turning to himself as a self-sufficient being, takes away the light in which he sees. Man is left gazing about in darkness, standing and seeing himself and his world in a peculiar twilight. It is this twilight that hides from man the fatal character of such an egoistic and autonomous existence; that deceivingly presents to him the egoistic and autonomous existence as the desired life; and that leads him away from the truth, away from the obvious and genuine reality of things, himself and his world, away into confusion and error.

Such is man as he passes down through history since Adam. Under pressure from the autonomous spirit of the world and out of aversion for God the creator whom he will not thank for the gift of himself and his world, man disavows his life. He refuses to give himself to God, because by rejecting God man can create the illusion of a life which consists in doing what he pleases. But in reality, the only thing man thereby achieves is death.

But what force sets in motion this egoistic devotion to the sweep of the autonomous world? In answering this question, Paul proposes a set of circumstances that proves to him the enormous might of sin in this world since Adam, a might which we are forever minimizing. The force which provides the impetus to sin and death is the law. For Paul the law, briefly, is the claim which the creator advances. By this claim he directs his creatures to themselves and to their neighbors; in this way he directs his creatures to life and sustains them in this life. Paradigmatically this claim of God is revealed in the law of Israel; but he also speaks, sporadically of course and open to misinterpretation, in the conscience of the pagan. This claim is the word of the creator commanding a response by way of responsibility from each man, which word alone keeps the life of the world in tow. But how?

Is this law the force which provokes man to sin unto death, and which plays him and his world into the hands of the autonomous spirit of the world? In reality St. Paul thinks so, and one can check his meaning in Romans 7 and Galatians 3. It is certainly not the fault of God the creator that the law has such an effect on the world of Adam; nor does the fault lie with his command. It also does not lie in the possibility that the powers and sin may have destroyed the law. On the contrary, the claim of the creator and of his creation endures in the midst of this world of sin unto death, this world which lies in the sway of death. The fault lies in the might of the powers and of sin. "The law [the claim of the creator] is holy, and the command [its particular decree] is holy, just and good," says St. Paul (Rom. 7:12).

But the self-seeking of man and the self-assertive spirit which inspires him cause this claim of God and his decrees, coming to us in the context of the world and history, to encounter and use man in such a way that the claim only drives man to self-assertion, self-assurance and self-edification. The reaction of man to the law is this: either he transgresses one commandment after the other and he is unjust, or he fulfils only the letter of the commandment in order thereby to reassure and glorify himself. The commandment then becomes an impulse to self-righteousness. It makes no difference for the whole of human history that, amidst this constant provocation by the law misused by sin, there is an occasional fulfilment of the commandments. The seeking of self takes control of the law in such a way that the law ends up serving this self-seeking, this egoism, and thereby serves death. "And the commandment that was unto life was discovered in my case to be unto death" (Rom. 7:10).

Since the powers and men make the law of life into a law of death, it is no wonder that within their closed-up world the fundamental attitude is one of hostility—hostility toward God and toward one another. Where man consistently yields in every novel way to the tendency of egoistic self-assertion inaugurated by Adam, and where he sees and understands God and every other man either as a hindrance or as a means to his own self-assertion, there can be basically no peace.

The reality of life in which we now find ourselves is an incessant struggle between creation and the powers and men. Creation is not destroyed by the fall of the powers and men; it is not fatally hurt. God the creator is not vanquished or crippled; he will preserve his creation up to that moment which he has determined. But creation is opposed and despoiled by the powers and men, and is, as St. Paul puts it, subjugated to "vanity." In the vain falsehood of their self-seeking hearts and of their self-assertive appearance, men seek to "make vain," to frustrate, God's work of creation.

III

But God does not desert his fallen creation; he restores it. He intervenes once again in his creation, which throughout its history since Adam has disavowed its creator. He fulfils the destiny which he gave it, and which it also had as creation. He leads it anew into obedience, placing it under the dominion of Christ.

How does this come about? St. Paul answers: by the cross and the resurrection of Christ. This formula goes back to apostolic times. For most of us it is a rather well-worn formula, but in it is proclaimed the historical event which breaks through this dimension of world and existence. Through this formula are proclaimed that God gives the world and men a new beginning and that he does this by means of a historical action taking place in their own history. His manifold wisdom, already hidden in creation, is introduced into the world in a concrete man, in a concrete historical place, at a concrete historical time—namely, in Jesus Christ.

God is now, as Paul says, "at work in Christ" (Eph. 1:20). He is at work in the cross of Christ. For on the cross we see at a glance where the whole history of Jesus Christ leads. The cross determines his history from the very beginning, and as foundation and goal it intrinsically determines his every act. On the cross is realized a steadfast obedience to the Father within a world introverted and turned away from him. On the cross, amidst the self-seeking and self-centered world, culminates that disinterested openness of self toward others in obedience to the precept of God. On the cross and in his death on the cross,

Christ's obedient acceptance of the will of God and the conscious taking-in-hand of the fatal claims of selfish men reach fulfilment.

On the cross, in his obedience to God, we see the expiation of the deadly sins of others, which have been taken into his own existence (into his own body!). In a very concrete sense, the cross is the taking-upon-himself by Christ of other men's claim to life in renunciation of his own claim; it is the obedient surrender of his own life for his neighbor. In this sense, therefore, the cross of Christ is the concrete breakthrough of the fallen world, a world dissipated by its egoistic pretensions. The cross is thus the divine beginning of a new obedient world in Christ.

But all this emerges in the resurrection of Jesus Christ from the dead. God thereby snatched from death into life him who had obediently taken upon himself the sin of others and caused it to die in his own death. Through the resurrection of Christ from the dead, God has showed that the power at work in the obedient love of Christ's sacrifice is more powerful than all the powers. For these powers have their might in death. A new beginning, a new just and true life now lie open for men in the crucified and risen Christ, who in the power of God has been raised up to the right hand of God, and in whose love the sin of others was made to die. A new possibility is now opened to all in the new reality of the crucified and risen Christ.

Men and the world are now once again aligned to Christ, from whose sacrifice they receive life. By the cross and the resurrection from the dead, Christ has now taken possession of his dominion. It is as Paul wrote to the community at Rome: "None of us lives to *himself* and none dies to *himself*; for if we live, we live to the *Lord,* or if we die, we die to the *Lord*. Therefore, whether we live or die, we are the Lord's. For it is to this end that Christ died and rose again, that he might be the Lord both of the dead and the living."

That Christ is the Lord is proven by the fact that the entire future decides itself upon him; or rather, he decides the entire future. Even when man wants to avoid Christ and his cross—and often an entire life is such an attempt to avoid him—even then man encounters nothing other than the Lord. Even when the world does not want to live any longer by the gift of the cross and resurrection, but wants rather to live according to the achievements which it can produce itself, its future is still the Lord and his conquering cross.

For St. Paul proclaims—along with the other sacred writers and the Lord himself—that the resurrection of the crucified Christ is indeed a resurrection that ends only with the parousia, with the manifest and definitive arrival of the glorified Lord. Whether we know it or not, whether we like it or not, the future for which we live, for which we all hope and therefore from which we all live, is in the hands of him who through the cross and resurrection has been empowered to be its Lord. Upon him our life depends now and depended then: it depends upon him now because it depended upon him then.

IV

For this reason, then, God's work in Christ, by which he shattered the shackles of sin and death, is not yet completed at the present moment of history. In the same power he used to raise Christ from the dead and glorify him above all the powers, God now prepares in Christ his definitive dominion; that is, Christ erects this dominion provisionally on earth—in the Church. In the same power: this is the power of the Holy Spirit. In this power of the Spirit, God has called Christ out of the darkness of death into light and life. In this power of the Spirit, he causes his life and light to go out over the world and into the hearts of men. This is no metaphor; it is an actual fact.

In order to further his dominion over the world in the Church, the crucified, risen and glorified Lord reveals himself to his apostles. He opens *himself* up to them and he opens *them* up to himself, in order that through them he may open himself to other men and other men to himself. This all takes place in the power of the Holy Spirit, who makes Christ known. In the Spirit, who discloses him and makes him present, Christ takes possession of those whom he sends, and authorizes them in their missionary activity with his word and deed. The apostles, authorized by his Spirit, enable Christ to enlighten and revive the hearts of the Jews and Gentiles; the apostles enable them to turn toward him and assemble around him as his people. In this his assembled people they enable him to emerge as in his body; in this his body, the Church, they enable him to reveal his dominion.

The letters of St. Paul bear witness to how concretely he understands the erection of the dominion of the crucified and risen Christ by means of the apostolic activity of the gospel in the Church. Christ himself, by the power that causes him to be present and to act—namely, in the Holy Spirit—makes use of the words and deeds of the apostles in order to reveal himself.

Through their words and deeds he reveals his history, his person, his word, his work, his suffering and death, his resurrection and ascension, his second coming. He addresses men and draws near to them. In the light of his truth Christ lays bare to men their muddled, confused lives. He shows them their new foundation based on his sacrifice and opens to them a just and justified life based on God's act of grace and forgiveness in him. He allows men to descry the endless view from the cross. In the power of the Holy Spirit and through the apostolic preaching, exhortation, and offer of himself, Christ draws men into his domain. His domain, the place where he is present in the world, is the Church.

We can sum all this up in a phrase: through the apostolic *word and deed*. We thereby capture in the words of Paul himself what he considers the "gospel": Christ's manifold word in proclamation, teaching, exhortation, precept, command, ordinance and prayer. But in the midst of the manifold word there are also efficacious signs, above all baptism and the Eucharist: that all-encompassing word, the most intensive and efficacious of words, which causes him to be efficaciously present in a sign.

And accompanying and confirming all this we have what Paul calls "signs and miracles": God's wonderful acts of power in extraordinary charisms which stir up faith in the gospel. Finally in the service of all these realities is the apostolic existence, the suffering in his apostolic following, in which the Lord's cross is visibly apparent. "For we the living are constantly being handed over to death for Jesus' sake, that the life also of Jesus may be made manifest in our mortal flesh" (2 Cor. 4:11).

But there is more: we speak of the *apostolic* word and work. And in reality it is the apostle himself who in a fundamental and authentic way makes accessible in word and deed the dominion of Christ in the Holy Spirit. We can see already in the letters of St. Paul that the apostolic word and deed continue in the word and deed of the Church. And the Church, on the foundation of the apostles and prophets whose word and deed she unfolds, pours out the apostolic patrimony until the end of time. As is stated in Ephesians 4:16: "For from him (the head) the whole body . . . derives its increase to the building up of itself in love."

Even more important in our context is to see as a whole the one great movement in which the world has been engaged since the cross and resurrection of Christ. This movement even now leads men and their world—both of which are capable of being brought into line again with Christ—to him and keeps them centered upon him in the assembly of his people, in the membership of his body, the Church. This movement begins when Jesus Christ, in the power of the life-giving Spirit, calls the sinful world out of death and into the power of God. It continues in the present world by the call of the Lord to his provisional dominion through the apostolic activity of the gospel, again in the power of the same Spirit. It will end when the Lord, "on command" from the Father, makes his re-entry in the parousia and definitively manifests his dominion in himself and in his own. But even before this movement was set in motion by the cross and resurrection, it began in the design and designation of the world by God for Christ, for whom God had indeed prepared creation.

V

But how is Christ's provisional dominion over his own realized? Here, where the nature of his dominion must be reflected in the mirror of Christian existence, we can give only a few indications. St. Paul, always in accord with the other apostolic writers, stresses that the glorified Lord brings himself to word and ear by means of the gospel. He becomes the Lord because we hear him, because we become obedient to him and thus belong to him. This attentive obedience is what Paul calls faith. Paul passionately defended the concept of faith against the misunderstanding of the Jews and Gentiles, who saw it as an achievement of action or thought.

Yet faith is not an achievement, but a decision: the decision of one who hears Christ impelling him to obedience. In such a decision faith does an about-face. It turns away, as Paul says, from its earlier idols (among whom we can reckon man himself as the most intimate and fascinating); it turns toward the "service of the living and true God" (1 Thess. 1:9). In faith man makes a decision about himself. In faith he enters into the dominion of God in Christ. Faith is a continually renewed surrender to the Lord to whom we belong.

In both of these aspects faith is, of course, only the beginning of the new life under the dominion of Christ. This dominion is made firm in love, for love is the energy of faith. Love is the proof that in faith Christ's life is given to me from the hand of God. Love is the effective answer to Christ's word of love which has again opened up to me an existence for God and for my neighbor; it consists in keeping my life open to God and to my neighbor. In the justice and truth of love, our neighbor also experiences this openness of life.

If love is the exercise of faith, then hope is faith's aim and impulse. Hope is the confident abandonment to the perspective opened to it in Christ. Hope encourages and strengthens the trust which, in spite of the pressure of realities in the foreground, soberly keeps vigil for that which is both invisible and to come. Hope enkindles the expectation of the life proclaimed and proffered in Christ; it waits for Christ with eager longing (cf. Rom. 8:19).

On the one hand, hope pushes to him in advance of all time; while the hopeless—because always disappointing—seeking of self is always running about behind time, even though it is "up-to-date," or rather precisely because it is "up-to-date." On the other hand, hope waits in patience. It anticipates nothing presumptuously, not even death or the frightening power of the cosmos. Meanwhile, the man who holds fast to himself and to an autonomous world loses himself in the illusions of an impatience evidently justified in his own eyes. Thus hope is seen looking toward Christ, projecting itself toward him who is to come. Hope hurries on and yet waits right there where there is nothing more to hope for: in the afflictions of life, in persecution, in death; hope shows itself in patience, which undergoes death as both death and life.

We must cut short these considerations. It may also be clear how the dominion of the crucified and risen Christ comes about and is reflected in actual Christian existence—in faith, hope and love and in all that these entail. For in faith, hope and love, man not only lives on the strength of the claim of the cross and resurrection of Christ, but enters into this claim and at the same time into the very cross and resurrection itself. In these virtues, on the basis of the cross and resurrection of Christ, man finally lets go of himself in abandonment to God and to the one whom God sends together with his claims. In faith, hope, love, patience and the other virtues, man accepts the new foundation of his life and begins to live again from the power of God: in, with and under Christ.

Man thereby accomplishes only the basic outline of his life, which his baptism has already sketched for him. "For we were buried with him by means of baptism into death, in order that, just as Christ has arisen from the dead through the glory of the Father, so we also may walk in the newness of life" (Rom. 6:3). Since the Christian follows the pattern of life delineated for him in baptism, he allows the design which Christ has marked out in the world to appear prominently in him. He witnesses in his being and existence the cross and resurrection of Christ as the foundation and goal of his life. He thus gives witness to the dominion of Christ over his own.

VI

We have seen that Christ is Lord over his own to the point of inserting them into his cross and resurrection. But the question remains: just what does this dominion over his own, his provisional dominion in the Church, mean for the world? By "world" we do not mean here the environment of Christians. Were we to mean that, then the only answer could be that this dominion signifies the liberation of this world to a new and yet old order: liberation looking toward the re-establishment of creation in Christ. Where faith, hope and love reign in a community and determine its spirit, there also the original truth, justice, the holiness of things, the health and harmony of creation become visible.

By "world" we do not, therefore, mean the milieu which surrounds the Church. We rather have in mind the non-Christians and their environment: the men and masses, as Paul says, "without." And we have in mind also a second reality: the powers and principalities which—and we must never forget it—also belong to the total reality of the world.

This world and the men "without" are, of course, also under the claim of the cross and resurrection of Christ. It is for them also that Christ has in his body taken away sin and death, and in his life makes ready a new life for them. This claim has become very concrete and historical for them through the appearance of the Church in the world. For what other reason has God, according to Paul, "even when we were dead by reason of our sins, brought us to life together with Christ . . . and raised us up together, and seated us together in heaven in Christ Jesus" except that "he might show in the ages to come the overflowing riches of his grace in kindness towards us in Christ Jesus" (Eph. 2:4 ff.)?

Now since Christ's death and resurrection, and since the head has formed a body, the Church, for himself in the world, there looms on the horizon of the future no further aeon, no further era of history, which does not have its eyes riveted on the sight of the grace manifested in the Church. The Church, by its appearance in the world and likewise in the heavens which determine the world, and by its appearance amidst the principalities and powers, draws the attention of all future times to itself. The Church is the great surprise, the great thorn in the side, the great invitation, the great hope of cosmic times.

Through the Church, the place and sign of grace, the question of grace is posed for all time, continually and everywhere: Will the world enter into this vital sphere which opens toward God and which renders life open toward God; or will it close itself off in its own sphere from the future, from Christ? Through the medium of the Church, the place of grace which Christ has won for himself and fulfilled, all history is called to let itself be fulfilled and thus to become fulfilled history. To that end the faithful themselves must do their utmost to show forth a life which has been fulfilled by grace.

The principalities and powers, as St. Paul calls them, also enter into the composition of the world. They are the deployments of that hostile spirit, of the autonomous force, which imperceptibly and unfathomably is at work in the world and which dominates its atmosphere. They are the deployments of that powerful and impalpable spirit which utilizes the world, its institutions, its persons and also its elementary powers, and in and through them effects its own destructive might.

They also, thanks to the Church, experience the new countenance of the wisdom of God. But they do not experience this new countenance as men do: men are faced with a decision; the powers experience the grace which shines forth in the Church as their judgment. For it belongs to their very essence to establish themselves in their own power, to be powers, that is, hostile powers, because they want to be autonomous powers. They are no longer capable of conversion. For them the cross and resurrection toll the end of their being, which now has nothing further to look forward to but annihilation. They see in the Church that the power of God is in Christ the victor, who triumphs over the autonomous powers. They discover through the Church that in Christ they are powerless.

But of course outside the Church and the dominion of Christ, where men withdraw themselves from his dominion, there the powers now strive more than ever to make a foothold. Thus history is traversed by an increasingly corrosive force hostile to Christ and his Church. At the same time—and this is a kind of self-affirmation of the powers, in fact the most dangerous kind—this force multiplies the imitations of the Spirit and of the very institution and structure of the Church to the point that short-sighted people, that is, those who cannot distinguish among the spirits, are unable to distinguish worldly utopias from eschatological hope, social society from the community of love, the *corpus humanum* from the *corpus Christi*.

The deceitful and lying miracles and signs of the antichrist, behind which lies the hostile spirit, are mentioned not only in the Apocalypse, but also by St. Paul (cf. 2 Thess. 2:9; 2 Cor. 11: 14). The fear of the future, in which Christ is to be revealed as the master of the powers and the powers exposed as devoid of power, so enrages these powers against one another and against the Church, that Paul, rejecting all deceptive hope both from within and from without the Church, speaks of the time since Christ as the "evil days." Paul adds further that these "evil days" proceed inexorably toward "the evil day" which circumscribes and completes them.

In view of this day, when the dominion of Christ over his own will once again be put to the test by a general attack from the exacerbated powers, it is important, as Paul says, to gird ourselves with the full armor of God. This certainly does not protect the "soldiers of Christ" from suffering and death, and it does not prepare them for a victory on earth; but it does preserve them from eternal ruin and causes them to remain steadfast to God.

St. Paul knows that God has selected and predestined Christ alone as the Lord of the world; that from all time God had already ordered creation to Christ as the future Lord; that God established him in this dignity through the cross and resurrection. Paul knows that Christ has provisionally erected his dominion in the world in the Church; that this incites the spirit of the autonomous world—that spirit which has nothing to gain and everything to lose—against this dominion; and that these days, the evil days of our time, are heading irrevocably toward Christ's future, the definitive and revealed emergence of his dominion. Paul knows the anguish and yet the consolation of this world-situation, and in unambiguous language he discloses what he knows to his fellow Christians. That is why he tells them from the beginning: "Let us be watchful and sober" (1 Thess. 5:6).

The Eucharist as Symbol of the Consecration of the World

by WALTER DÜRIG

THE FIRST CHAPTERS of the Bible give a vivid description of the way in which God created the world. According to this account, God created one part of the world after another and united the parts in an orderly whole. We are told, in the dramatic style of the old epics, how in a single week God created the firmament, the air, the earth and stars, the birds and the beasts that crawl on the ground, and man himself; the work was completed in six days. The description ends with this summary: "Thus the heavens and the earth were finished and all their array. On the sixth day God finished the work he had been doing. And he rested on the seventh day from all the work he had done" (Gen. 2:1 ff.). Thanks to modern exegesis, today we need no more than mention that the biblical account of creation does not pretend to be an exact, literal expression of scientific facts.

I. CREATION

In his narrative, expressed in a childlike, popular form but suited at the same time for liturgical use, the inspired author wants to show that the whole world is God's handiwork. Through God's creating word the world was raised out of nothingness and formed into a cosmos. As each portion of the history of creation is completed, the narrative emphasized that what God made was good, that it was very good (Gen. 1:31). Again, there is nothing scientific said about the world or its pragmatic usefulness. "Good" here means participation in the goodness of God, who has thought and willed every created thing.

Thus when the Bible calls creation good, it reveals that the world, which is good as a whole and in all its parts, reflects God's perfection, and that God sees his own perfections in the world. Bound to God by their inner nature and by their deepest being and meaning, material objects are the glorious reflection of God, whose invisibility is clothed in the world as in a garment. The things of the world, like pictures pregnant with God's revelation, proclaim the spirit and love that dwell in God from all eternity.

In the account of creation, it is clear that the world was created as a cosmos, that is, that creatures of every sort do not exist in isolation, only for themselves, but rather stand in a real order and inner *connected*ness to one another. Inorganic creation has meaning for living things and the latter in turn for spiritual creatures. The creator made the life of plants and lower animals come forth from inorganic matter because he wanted these things to be intrinsically connected.

Revelation further describes an inner connection between nature and spirit, a union of higher beings with lower ones. The idea of the creation of the world is therefore concerned with *realizing* the unity and connectedness of everything and *spirit*ualizing the world so that it is God's image and tool, a deeply meaningful book of symbols written in expressive picture-language. The reflected splendor of God's power and beauty shines forth in the tangible forms of the created universe, which despite its multiplicity is invisibly interconnected through the different creatures' inner relationship to the same creator.

In accordance with this basic law of unity, a connection also exists between the world with its elements, forces and qualities on the one hand, and supernatural goods on the other. In biblical prehistory the elements, rivers, mountains, light and color, stone and metal, plants and animals are the symbols and tools of spiritual powers and goods. The fountain of Paradise signifies grace; the snake is the devil; the tree and its fruit refer to knowledge and life. In Old Testament spirituality, the cloud is the sign of God's nearness; the animal symbolizes the angelic spirit. In Jewish worship, water, oil, resin, bread, wine, the distinction between clean and unclean animals—all point darkly and enigmatically to an inner connection between the order of creation and the order of grace. Hermann Schell expresses this divine mystery of creation in these words: "Right from the beginning nature was a great sacrament of grace, a transparent symbol of the spiritual world of ideas, an effective means of spiritual anointing." [1]

II. INCARNATION

The world has been contaminated by sin. Something inimical to God, or at least strange to him, has forced its way into it. "For creation was made subject to vanity—not by its own will but by reason of him who made it subject—in hope, because creation itself also will be delivered from its slavery to corruption into the freedom of the glory of the sons of God. For we know that all creation groans and travails in pain until now" (Rom. 8:20–22).

Through sin man has condemned the world to corruption and has made worldly values deceptively autonomous. Here in this false autonomy lies the creature's real nothingness, which man has brought about. This nothingness appears primarily in the misuse of created goods. But the world is not totally corrupt. As God's handiwork the things of the world are still bound to him in their very existence; the creature longs for transfiguration, that is, for the bond with God deep within it to come to the surface.

This longing of creation began to be objectively fulfilled in that instant when the Son of God was united to his human nature in Mary's womb. Christ's human nature "is made from a daughter of Adam and Eve, and therefore the germ of it is already contained in Adam and Eve, in a biological union with the whole human race. Humanity in its material-physiological existence is nothing other than the unfolding of Adam's life. Because of this oneness of the human race, all men stand in a real relationship to Christ's human nature, which sprang from man. Moreover, his human nature, even though directly and essentially entrusted with God's own life, was not torn away from the race. Now in its materiality, Christ's human nature is also dust from the dust of the world and is thereby related to the other material parts of the universe: Christ's humanity remains ever and always bound up with the universe, both spiritually and materially." [2]

Through the fact of the incarnation, the world's close relationship to God is intensified in an essentially new way, quite beyond anything that can be conceived through faith in God's act of creation. God's love is not content simply with the act of creation, through which all creatures are of course his handiwork but are not yet united to him in their essence. Because the Son of God has entered into the matter of this world and because he has taken on the flesh and blood of Adam's children, God's glory takes real shape in the material world, and his essential union with creation, unhindered even by man's sin and corruption, becomes visible.

Inasmuch as Christ's human nature is not isolated from man or the universe, but rather remains closely related to the human race and the whole of creation, the world becomes even more closely connected to God than it was when it was created. Because of this real connectedness, Christ's life, the only true life in the world, can also become the life of the world.

III. CONSECRATION OF THE WORLD

With the words from the Martyrology, *"mundum volens adventu suo piissimo consecrare"* ("wanting to sanctify the world through his obedient coming"), the Church proclaims on Christmas Eve that the whole world is called in the incarnation to Christ's life. Anyone who genuinely celebrates the Church's Christmas liturgy must reject the poetry about the sweet baby Jesus and the "pretty little boy with the curly hair" and acknowledge with the Church the beginning of the consecration of the world, which commences in that instant when God lays his hand on the world in the incarnation of his Son and makes it again his own, more intensely than in creation. The consecration of the world, which began when the Lord came in the fullness of grace, gives the material world a new meaning in its relationship to Christ's humanity, so that material objects can bear and transmit not only the meaning which is theirs from creation, but also divine life.

The consecration of the world—the absorption of man and the universe into Christ's life—is clearly taught in the New Testament. "In him [Christ] were created all things in the heavens and on the earth, things visible and things invisible . . . All things have been created through and unto him, and he is before all creatures, and in him all things hold together. . . . For it has pleased God . . . that . . . through him he should reconcile to himself all things, whether on the earth or in the heavens" (Col. 1:16–20).

Paul says this even more clearly in Ephesians 1:9 f.: God made known to us "the mystery of his will according to his good pleasure. And this his good pleasure he purposed in him to be dispensed in the fullness of the times: to re-establish all things in Christ, both those in the heavens and those on the earth." The rendering of this text in the Vulgate as *"instaurare omnia in Christo"* and its English translation as "restore," "renew" or "re-establish" "all things in Christ" should not lead us to pervert its original sense or limit it to the realm of mere ethics. The Apostle is first and foremost interested in the *anakephalaiosis,* the recapitulation, that is, in renewing and summarizing the whole spiritual and material universe.[3] The ethical *instauratio,* the renewal of man's moral actions through the observance of Christ's laws, is both a prerequisite and an effect of the *anakephalaiosis.*

According to a statement of Pius XII, every baptized man must work "to transform the whole world from the ground up, to change it from a savage world to a humanly noble one, from a humanly noble world to a consecrated one." Every age, every state of life, every vocation has the obligation to proclaim in its own situation, work and actions the consecration of the world that has already begun in Christ's incarnation so that the world may be transfigured, that is, healed and perfected in Christ's glory. Every Christian, that is, everyone who applies to himself this title taken from Christ's divine office, binds himself thereby to help bring Christ's work to perfection, namely, to gloriously renew himself, humanity and the world.

IV. THE EUCHARIST

The whole universe has "its existence in Christ": this is the fundamental testimony of revelation about the universe. Christ is the fulfilment of all cosmic and human becoming. This relationship to Christ gives the universe new meaning and luster. Created spirit and matter receive the guarantee of indestructible existence in that moment when they enter into a real, corporeal connection with Christ's life. When the believer acknowledges that the sacrament of the altar is Jesus Christ's true body and blood, he gains a deeper and more complete understanding of the relationship between God and the world which he experiences through faith in the incarnation of the Son of God.

Nowhere but in the eucharistic bread and wine can the Christian see so tangibly and so clearly that all life here on earth is fulfilled in Christ. One may characterize the Eucharist as symbolic of the consecration of the world precisely because God's continual intervention in the world to fill it anew with his own life is particularly striking in the eucharistic presence of the Son of God under the appearances of bread and wine. Like every true symbol, it uncovers yet covers at the same time, since it expresses not its own existence but another's—indeed, in the form of a symbol.[4]

It is in the Eucharist that bread and wine, representing the universe, become able to bear and to mediate divine, eternal life; for this reason the Eucharist is a symbol of the consecration of the world. What natural forces have prepared is lifted up to the everlasting glory of Christ's body and blood. In the Eucharist, life on earth reaches its highest peak; created life is perfected. What the world has gained in the incarnation of the Son of God and how thoroughly the universe, doomed to corruption because of sin, has been elevated through him become clear in the consecrated bread and wine. The world in which natural objects like bread and wine can become Christ's body and blood and thereby bear divine life is called home to communion with the Eternal Word and thus to learn the secret of the inner life of the Trinity. The Eucharist manifests and pledges the fulfilment of the creature's longing for transfiguration.

Furthermore, the Eucharist is a symbol of the consecration of the world because not only the representatives of material things but also man's very work gains new meaning in it. Bread and wine are produced not only by natural forces but also by human labor. The primary sense of man's labor is most clearly preserved in bread and wine: inasmuch as only bread and wine are put on the altar and integrated into Christ's sacrifice, all the toil of our daily work ends in glory and everlasting life, in Christ's body and blood.

Thus we see that the deepest meaning and purpose in our work is to form the Eucharist, to *realize* the Lord's body in the forms of the world. Whether we give the fruit of our labors as bread and wine or as money is of secondary importance. What matters is that all our toil and trouble, our hopes and expectations enter into Christ's body in the Eucharist and are taken up into God's glory.

Because the Eucharist as food becomes one with him who eats it, it transforms not only man's work, but also his being. It is a law of physiology that an organism of a higher order assimilates lower ones. Thus when a man receives the Eucharist, he does not transform Christ into himself, but is himself transformed into Christ. "He who eats my flesh and drinks my blood abides in me and I in him. As the living Father has sent me, and as I live because of the Father, so he who eats me, he also shall live because of me" (John 6:57 f.).

The Fathers of the fourth century had already integrated this central thought into their discussion of the plan of salvation. They continually stress that God became man in the incarnation and unites himself with man in the Eucharist so that man might become godlike. Leo the Great says: "The effect of receiving Christ's body and blood is that we are transformed into what we eat." The idea that the Eucharist is merely food for the soul is unknown to patristic theology, which strongly emphasizes that the Eucharist nourishes and maintains the whole man with his unity of body and soul, and for this reason is a pledge of the glorious resurrection of the body. In the Eucharist the whole man experiences the salvation wrought by the Son of God, who became flesh to lead all flesh to the glory of his resurrection.

If we consider, however, that we have in the Eucharist the living bread which in the words of Holy Scripture is given "for the life of the world," we must then conclude that the Eucharist does not symbolize merely the consecration of material nature or of someone's individual existence and work; it symbolizes much more the consecration of humanity as a whole. The power of Christ's life, which is given to us in the consecrated bread and wine, maintains and strengthens the community of those who believe in Christ and forms them into one body, Christ's body. "Because the bread is one, we though many are one body, all of us who partake of the one bread" (1 Cor. 10:17).

It would be a great mistake to overvalue the Eucharist's power to form a community (that is, its power to give birth to a community) and to forget the axiom which is valid even here: *gratia supponit naturam*. The Eucharist is the sacrament of community primarily in the sense that it feeds and glorifies the community: in a mystical, sacramental way it truly forms the community of man that already exists in the body of Christ. The Secret of the Mass for Corpus Christi must be understood in this sense: "We beg you, O Lord, graciously grant your Church the gifts of unity and peace, which are represented by the gifts that we have offered."

The pastoral letter of the German bishops preparing for the Eucharistic Congress (in 1960) rightly states: "The principle of life in the Church is not primarily a human accomplishment, but rather one of the grace of God." It stresses at the same time, however, that "the religious success of the Congress must be obtained in God's grace through prayer and sacrifice." As before every eucharistic gathering, the individual grain of wheat must fall to the earth and die; otherwise it remains alone. Without this the Eucharist— which is the way in which we help perfect Christ's work by consecrating the world and gloriously reforming our own selves, humanity, and the world in the final, mighty "recapitulation"— becomes for the individual and the community an empty form.

NOTES

[1] H. Schell, *Dogmatik III*, pp. 1, 442.

[2] J. Pinsk, *Die sakramentale Welt* (Freiburg: 1941), pp. 20 f.

[3] Cf. H. Schlier in Kittel's *Theologisches Wörterbuch zum NT III*, pp. 681 f.

[4] A further study of the symbolism of the liturgy may be found in W. Dürig, *Imago* (Munich: 1952).

The Meaning of Christ's Parousia for the Salvation of Man and the Cosmos

by Leo Scheffczyk

AN ADEQUATE UNDERSTANDING of the second coming of Christ is possible only if the location of this particular truth at the juncture of three other truths is taken into consideration. These other truths are: an awareness of the historical nature of the accomplishment of redemption; the conviction that in Christ the *eschaton* (the end or final age) has already come; and the recognition that the accomplishment of redemption is total and universal, excluding no realm of the created world.

The first truth indicates that salvation is accomplished in a context that is both vital and active, demanding of man his own free decision and affirmation. The second points out that the decisive act of salvation has already taken place, in Christ's incarnation and death, and that in Christ mankind's decision and option for this salvation have already been objectively reached. The third indicates that this decision has a reality about it that eliminates every possible created limitation: the Christ-event has unloosed a wave that will penetrate to all boundaries and then break through into the eternal.

Of course one must not overlook the fact that these three closely connected ideas have their foundation in the truth of that *eschaton* brought by Jesus Christ.[1] As the promised one he is the goal and meaning of the Old Testament as well as of all history; as the one who has come, he is the accomplishment and the end, which, however, simultaneously show themselves as a new beginning and make him recognizable as one who is still coming, the one who alone can fulfil all perfectly.

This central position of Christ in the doctrine of the supra-individual last things requires a consideration of the meaning of his first coming preliminary to a discussion of the meaning of his second coming in the plan of salvation. For it is out of this first coming that the meaning of the second unfolds and develops as the bloom and fruit of the bud.

I. THE INCARNATION OF CHRIST AS THE END-EVENT

To see that the appearance of God in human flesh, with death and resurrection, was the decisive moment of the history of salvation —indeed, that history thus reached its end objectively and, in one sense, ceased to be history—one must look at the Christ-event in the perspective of the Old Testament and its expectation of the end. This is the prophetic vision of the coming of the Messiah. According to this vision the Messiah will be the fulfilment of the longing of the nations, and hence the end of history will have been reached.

The act of creation itself, the beginning of Israel's history, bears witness to the intense eschatological character of Israel's understanding of itself and its history. For the Old Testament did not understand creation as a past, historical event. Rather, creation was viewed as the beginning of Yahweh's powerful activity with his people and mankind. This activity of Yahweh was always present in continual creative acts. It also had in its inner nature the potency of a new act of creation which would bring everything to its fullest perfection.

The description of the exodus from Egypt (Ps. 77; 106:19; Is. 51:9 ff.; Ez. 29:3) or of the return from the Babylonian exile (Is.

41:18; 43:18 f.) in terms of the creation story not only actualizes Israel's understanding of creation, but also gives it an eschatological color. Consequently the presentation of creation itself receives eschatological relevance. This is evident in those passages which describe the final events as a new creation,[2] in which God the creator appears as both destroyer and constructor of his work. Because Yahweh is creator in a perfect sense, he must also be the redeemer of the people (Is. 45:6 f.) and their definitive saviour (Is. 41:4). Thus the final and complete redemption of Israel can again be described in such a way that the original creation of paradisiac life is recalled (Is. 41:18-20). Hence it is quite clear that the Old Testament regards creation and fulfilment as correlative terms —the beginning of time and the end of time correspond.[3]

In post-Davidic times this interpretation of history,[4] which looks to the victory of God over enemy powers and to the fulfilment of creation, is united with the eschatological figure of the Messiah, the "anointed of Yahweh," the new David who will rule over Israel eternally as the king of the future (Ez. 37:21 ff.).[5] However, this idea could give only partial expression to the eschatological expectations, since it was more and more interpreted in the terrestrial, political terms of Jewish nationalism (the Psalms of Solomon and the Apocalypses of Esdras and Baruch). For this reason, in certain esoteric circles of Judaism[6] (4 Esdras and the Ethiopian Book of Henoch), a new name for the Messiah began to win favor, prompted by Daniel's vision (Dan. 7), namely, the Son of Man.

This Son of Man (Dan. 7:13) is (in a characteristic fusion of the collective and individual) the figure of the eschatological redeemer. His coming will cause a radical crisis in world-history; he will end the hegemony of the blasphemous powers and establish the messianic kingdom as a new creation from above.[7] In this way does the Old Testament indicate a step toward the messianic fulfilment, the hope of a singular new descent of God in which all history will reach its fulfilment.

The New Testament allows no doubt whatsoever that this hope was fulfilled with the coming of Christ. This is indicated above all by the fact that Jesus regarded himself in terms of the eschatological function of the Son of Man and applied this royal title to himself.[8] In his mouth the designation "Son of Man" was (in a remarkable continuation and development of the Old Testament usage) an expression of both royalty and fealty.

The royal character of this title is shown in the answer given to the high priest: "You shall see the Son of Man sitting at the right hand of the Power and coming with the clouds of heaven" (Mark 14:62). The aspect of lowliness, which was inspired by the Isaian "servant of Yahweh" theme, is revealed most clearly in Mark 10:45: "The Son of Man has not come to be served but to serve, and to give his life as a ransom for many." (Cf. also Mark 8:31.) However, both aspects confirm the consciousness of Jesus that the end of time has come for the world (Matt. 11:4 ff.; 12:28), that the decisive crisis has come, which he will so definitively turn to the good, and that in him and his work history has reached its goal.

In the vision of the prophets, the final crisis of history is often united with a dramatic judgment scene and joined to the "Day of Yahweh" (Am. 2:16; Is. 2:20; Mich. 2:4; and other passages). In the New Testament this eschatological presentation is applied to the Christ-event, especially to Christ's death and resurrection. There is already an indication of this in the way the Synoptic Gospels place the parousia statements of Jesus, which speak of the Day of Yahweh, before the history of the passion (Matt. 24; Mk. 13; Lk. 21). It is not by chance, then, that the passion narratives contain many elements which the parousia statements use to describe the Day of Yahweh (flight, persecution, cosmic catastrophes).[9]

In the parousia statements the decisive event was the coming of the Son of Man on the clouds of heaven. It is impossible not to see parallels in the descriptions of the resurrection of the Lord and his ascension into heaven (Lk. 24:51; Acts 1:9 ff.). The victorious character of the Day of Yahweh, which Christ brings into existence, is obvious in all these events. The disciples of Jesus as well as the early Christian communities could not but see in Christ by reason of the testimony of the Lord and their own conviction the fulfilment of the eschatological prophecies and the end of history.

Because it is with such vigor that the New Testament sees in Christ the fulfiller of history, the following question could easily arise: Did his coming and activity perhaps bring the time of salvation to a complete standstill and put an end to the movement of history completely? This opinion looks to the "proximate expectation" of the early Christians for its support. It is expressed in such theories as Dodd's "realized eschatology" [10] and Schweitzer's "consequent eschatology." [11]

However, neither theory does justice to the fact that even the Synoptic Gospels, in spite of this "proximate expectation," allow for the temporal duration of this "end" and for its further development of history. Jesus' use of the designation "Son of Man" points to a function of the present along with a task to be accomplished in the future.[12] The same point is indicated in the refusal of Christ to give any definite information about the end of time (Mark 13:32; Lk. 17:20).[13] Thus room is left for an interim time and age.

Finally, it seems that the whole question of the proximate or remote end (and the prophecies about such) results more from a certain philosophical consideration of time than from a genuine biblical mode of thought. In philosophy the consideration of time is concerned with the measurement of the before and after. Such a concept is not necessarily to be postulated of the Bible. In biblical thought the coming of Jesus was the Day of Yahweh, which indeed brings the end with it; but it is as a dawn in Christ and is to rise to the full light of noon.

II. CHRIST, MANKIND AND THE COSMOS

For the eschatological understanding of the Christ-event, the most important question is how Christ can be perceived not only as the temporal end of the actions of God in history, but also as the perfecter of all mankind, indeed, of all material creation.

The biblical witnesses maintain this fact with univocal certitude. Old Testament prophecy already clearly states that the final judgment as well as salvation includes the whole covenant people. Although the expectation of salvation may have been a particular one earlier (Osee 2:21), for Isaiah it has already become universal and pertains to all mankind. The picture of the pilgrimage of the nations (Is. 2:2 ff.) shows how all nations come to the mountain of God to be taught by the God of Jacob and to receive from him the eschatological gifts of justice and peace. Similarly, in the third part of the book of Isaiah, we read: "Nations shall behold your vindication, and all kings your glory" (Is. 62:2).

The great event at the end of time also includes and embraces the material cosmos. For the Old Testament this truth is the simple conclusion of the historical-eschatological understanding of the creative act at the beginning of time. Since Yahweh created the material world for a goal at the end of time, it must take part in the state of the final fulfilment in its own manner. It must also be affected by his powers and actions. Thus, the extrahuman world also takes part in the end-events.

In the Old Testament this truth is mentioned only in passing and unreflectively. It is contained implicitly in the clear and explicitly stated knowledge that man and the material world form a one-destiny community. And in this community the actions of man impress themselves on the cosmos. Old Testament man experienced this common destiny first of all in the tragedy of sin, which also brought the curse of God to nonhuman creation (Gen. 3:17; 5:29; Wis. 2:24; Rom. 5:12; 8:19 ff.).

The awareness of the relationship between the sins of mankind and the tribulations of creation is eloquently stated in the so-called apocalypse of Isaiah (Is. 24–27), where it receives its classical expression. Here, as elsewhere among the prophets (Joel 2:10; 4:15 f.; Jer. 4:24 ff.; Ez. 32:7), the fundamental connection between protology and eschatology is visualized above all in terms of non-salvation: because man has sinned and thereby desecrated creation, the latter must endure a catastrophe at the end of time, a catastrophe whose cause is Yahweh himself. "Behold, the Lord empties the land and lays it waste; he turns it upside down, scattering its inhabitants . . . The earth is utterly laid waste, utterly stripped" (Is. 24:1–3). This destructive force on the Day of Yahweh extends even to the stars and causes them to fall (Is. 34:4), so that the world finds itself in darkness (Is. 13:10; Jer. 4:23; Joel 2:2).

However, this communal destiny of man and the cosmos is also to be seen in terms of salvation. Here the redemption of man is continued in the transformation of the cosmos and in the creation "of a new heaven and a new earth" (Is. 65:17). The result of this transformation is the perfect condition and state of creation—peace among animals (Is. 11:6–9), and the disappearance of suffering (Is. 65:18 f.) and death (Is. 25:8)—often expressed in very earthly symbols.[14] While these insights may not be extremely clear, there can be no doubt that they express the belief that the material world is to share in the final redemption of mankind at the end of time.

This truth of the communal destiny of man and the cosmos, founded in protology and directed to eschatology, receives a much more explicit treatment in the New Testament. In Jesus' preaching, the last judgment and the gaining of immortal life are connected with the idea of the *paliggenesia* (Matt. 19:28 f.). Although nothing here is said directly about a cosmic transformation,[15] neither is this excluded as the necessary background.[16] The correspondence between human and cosmic fate at the end of time permeates especially the synoptic accounts of the parousia statements (Mk. 13; Matt. 24; Lk. 21).

Creation is also to share in the afflictions of the judgment passed on mankind. Correspondingly, it will also share in the redemption which the just will experience, and which is drawing near under the sign of natural catastrophes (Luke 21:28). This is hinted at in the statements about the parousia, where there is no mention of a complete destruction of the world,[17] although it must also be admitted that there is likewise no mention of a transformation of the world. However, the only possible background against which these statements could have been understood would have been the late Jewish idea of a transformation of the world in connection with catastrophes caused by the powers of nature.

This positive aspect is already hinted at in Matthew 17:11 (parallel in Mk. 9:12), where mention is made of Elias, who will "restore all things." This idea is quite explicit in the concept of *apokatastasis panton* in the Apocalypse (3:21). It is also clearly expressed in the idea of the "new heaven and new earth," which has its origin in the prophetic tradition and is taken up in the Apocalypse (21:15) and 2 Peter (3:13). It also appears in Pauline theology (Heb. 12:26 f.; Rom. 8:19-22; 1 Cor. 7:31; Eph. 1:9 f.; Col. 1:18-20).

In the New Testament presentation of the communal fate of human and cosmic being in the parousia of the Lord, the anthropological element of the new creation receives greater emphasis and eventually becomes the chief idea.[18] Thus the Apocalypse envisages the content of that which the new heaven and earth will establish as a community with God (Apoc. 21:7; 22:4). The second epistle of St. Peter (3:13) is chiefly concerned with that good of the perfect justice which will then be given to men. James 1:18 emphasizes especially that Christians are "first among his creatures." This indicates that the transformation of creation begins in the realm of man and grace and extends itself then to the whole world.

The same emphasis is to be found in St. Paul's concept of the *kaine ktisis* (2 Cor. 5:17). Consequently he evinces no great immediate interest in cosmological questions touching on the renewal of the world. (However, as Rom. 8:19 ff. shows, he does not deny familiarity with this aspect.)

In the New Testament this stronger centering of the renewal of the world in its anthropological aspect goes hand-in-hand with its closer connection with the Christ-event. This in turn makes the problem of the inner foundation of this community of destiny even more important for the theologian whose thought is based on the New Testament. According to the New Testament the further consequences of this common destiny are the result of the Christ-event, that is, the incarnation and death of Christ. Hence, the problem of the unity of all mankind becomes very pressing, for a transfiguration of the world through the coming of Christ, beginning with man and spreading out to the rest of creation, is possible only on the basis of the inner and essential unity of men with one another.

Otherwise it is not possible to understand how the Christ-event, the event and work of one man, can affect the whole of mankind. Until this is established, the extension of redemption to the cosmos cannot be broached. For this extension rests upon the supposition that the whole of mankind has been caught up in the saving act of Christ. Unless the essential unity of the human race is established, it is impossible to provide an adequate foundation for the third insight of Christian eschatology mentioned at the beginning of this essay, namely, the anthropological and cosmic universality of the work of Christ.

An awareness of the concrete, essential unity of the whole family of Adam belongs to the most fundamental data of the Bible, although the Bible does not treat this fact thematically and reflectively.

It is likewise one of the most fundamental of human insights, although it does not always attain a high degree of explicit and reflective consciousness on this level either. There is much truth in the statement that young children and wise old men are the most vitally aware of this fundamental truth of human nature.

However, this awareness has also found expression in many different ways in the workings of the human spirit. It lies behind Aristotle's doctrine that man has a social nature, as well as behind the categorical imperative of Kant. It is the decisive element in the Romantic thinking of mankind as an organic and living being. The modern world has arrived at the same insight along other ways and experiences: the discovery of the unconscious, in which the experience of long-passed generations is engraved; man's experience of the social consequences of human actions for both good and bad, especially in a world ever increasing in unity, both inwardly and outwardly; the knowledge that men depend on each other in the specialization and division of labor demanded by the technological age in which they now live.

All these factors have worked together to enliven once again modern man's awareness of this ancient truth: All men form such a coherent phylum, so united in itself by the hidden veins of humanity, that there is the most intimate communication among them —which, if not actual, is at least possible. Paul Claudel has given this newly found awareness its most impressive poetic expression. In his masterpiece, *The Satin Slipper,* the fate of individual man is no longer separable from the destiny of the whole world. This is especially evident in the chief protagonist, Rodrigo, "who belonged to those who can only save themselves by saving the whole group" (first scene).

Although this awareness of the unity of the whole family of man appears so universally accepted, its theoretical justification is not at all easy. The simplest basis is to be found in Platonic philosophy. For Platonic realism the ideas or essences of natural things are what really exist, before and apart from actual, individual things. Relations between these ideas and the individual things are constituted by means of participation or imitation. According to this theory, universal human nature exists as an essence before any individual men. These latter have their existence only through participation in the universal, real, and independently conceived human nature. Since this human nature is a single indivisible entity, every individual human carries this nature whole and entire in himself.

And thus man, in spite of his numbers, still makes up a strict unity, for in each individual the entirety of human nature is present. In this view the inclusion of all mankind in the redemption effected by the one man Jesus Christ is easily understandable. For mankind, even in its totality, was included in that one individual.

However, the great philosophical difficulties contained in Platonism must not be overlooked. Furthermore, Platonic dualism and devaluation of the corporeal generally hinder an adequate understanding of the unity of the human race. Hence an explanation based on the universality and unlimited nature of the human spiritual soul should provide a more convincing answer.

In its universal openness to all existence, the human soul contains all human perfections in itself potentially and virtually. Thus human existence is made into a common possession of all men. But, since the individual as such can realize this possession only in a limited manner, he is of necessity directed to and dependent upon all the others.[19] There arises a bond of unity from this need of the one for the others, of the dependence of the individual on all—and this bond is universal and inescapable.

This unity, based on one hand in the riches of universal openness and on the other in the poverty of dependence on one another, provides for unlimited communication of one man with another. As such, every deed of every individual must affect the whole, for good or bad, to its increase or decrease in perfection. Such an understanding of the unity of mankind offers an explanation of the ability of the act of the one man Jesus Christ to affect all mankind. And insofar as he was the God-man, he affects it in a singularly perfect way.

Compared with the proof for the inner unity of the human race, the clarification of man's unity with the cosmos offers no special difficulty. Common experience, especially of those men who live close to nature, shows that bodily man is lodged in infrahuman nature, that he is dependent upon it and intimately bound up with it. To these elementary considerations the Old Testament adds a religious and ethical truth: God gave the world to man at creation, as both gift and task (Gen. 1:28; Wis. 9:2).

On the basis of such a profound physical and moral unity with the cosmos, the fact that man could become the destiny of the cosmos is no longer surprising. The Old Testament points this out explicitly in its conception of the results of the fall and redemption (see above).

The Fathers of the Church added force to this natural bond of unity by their stoically inspired description of man as a microcosm. St. Basil the Great says that in himself man "sees the great wisdom of the Creator as in a microcosm" (Hom. Attend: PG 31, 216). For St. Ambrose "man also embodies summarily the universe" (Hexaem. 1, VI, 10, 75; PL 14, 288). The most detailed description of man as a microcosm dates from the ninth-century writings of the Greek patriarch Photius.[20]

Of course, the Fathers did not understand this unity of man with the universe in any crude physical sense, as if the cosmos were human or as if man were some sort of physical concentrate, an abridged edition of created reality. For them, rather, man is that being in which the meaning of the whole universe is centered and concentrated. Man is the synopsis of the idea and meaning of creation, and at the same time its original exemplar and real re-presentation. The cosmos has for this reason a real and actual presence within man, for man is the original form of creation and, as such, has a real-symbolic unity with all other forms.

This idea, the real-symbolic unity of man with the cosmos,[21] also points out the direction of the answer to the question about the basis of the unity between Christ, mankind and the whole cosmos. To say only that man is the meaning and thus the real-symbolic representative of creation does not fully satisfy either the Fathers of the Church or the biblical and theological thought about the meaning and goal of creation. The full (perfect) significance and meaning of creation are to be found only in the full (perfect) man. And such is the God-man Jesus Christ alone.

This truth is especially emphasized in the writings of Sts. Paul and John; it received its classical expression in the Christological hymn of the epistle to the Colossians, where St. Paul speaks of Christ: "He is the image of the invisible God, the firstborn of every creature. For in him were created all things in the heavens and on the earth, things visible and things invisible, whether Thrones or Dominations or Principalities or Powers. All things have been created through and unto him" (Col. 1:15 f.; cf. also 1 Cor. 8:6; Eph. 2:10; 3:9; Heb. 1:2 f.; Jn. 1:3 f.; Apoc. 3:14).

In this text Christ is described as the foundation, goal and original exemplar of creation and as the meaning which establishes the unity of all created things. Everything that exists is reduced to him as the principle of unity. Since Christ is the original foundation, center and goal of creation, the whole of mankind and of all infrahuman creation is perfectly represented in and by him, in whom it finds its unity. It is important to notice that Christ has this position not as *logos asarkos,* but as the God-man, even if his humanity had only an ideal existence before his incarnation.

The following conclusion is unavoidable: when this goal appeared in the world, as it was actualized and realized in the incarnation, death and resurrection of Christ, the whole of mankind and the cosmos had to be seized and caught up in it and transformed in its very roots. The redemption, which is the essence of the salvific meaning brought about in the coming of Christ, had to affect the whole human and infrahuman world in the man Christ. And beyond the forgiveness of sin, there would be the assimilation of man and the cosmos into the life and holiness of God. Wherever this would occur definitively and unsurpassably, there would the world have reached its goal in history and its end. And so the Christ-event, in its universal power and extension, actually brought all creation to its definitive state and being.

III. THE PROBLEM OF THE INTERIM TIME

A problem arises, however, when the Christ-event is so forcefully thought of as the end-event. And it was this problem that afflicted primitive Christianity in no small way. The problem is the question that automatically arises about the meaning of the time-in-between, the interim involved in the unfolding and development of the Christ-event in a first and second coming. In fact, how is a continuation of history beyond the fundamental end-event possible at all? God could have, of course, placed the end of all history in immediate conjunction with the death and resurrection of Christ. The objection that thus only a relatively small number of people would have enjoyed the great happiness of heaven overlooks the fact that the divine plan of salvation is not necessarily bound to some law of the greatest possible number. A deeper, more fitting reason must be found for the divine introduction of this interim period.

A more precise explanation of the redemptive act of Christ and its effects is now necessary. The organic unity between Christ and mankind (as well as the cosmos) voids any doubt about the immediacy and efficaciousness of Christ's redemptive act on humanity. The act of the God-man, the redeemer, gave his grace a permanent and definitive presence in the world. This transformed the world by changing its relationship to God, by drawing it definitively within the realm of God's mercy.

Thus mankind has received an existential and obligatory appointment and vocation to salvation. The human race cannot withdraw itself from this "given"; it must recognize it as pre-existent, whether it chooses to embrace it or not. This fact shows clearly that salvation chiefly reaches man objectively in the form of a powerful offer and call, and, as such, is already efficacious; at the same time it stands as mankind's vocation and task. This means quite simply: God so ordained the work of salvation that it can also be the work of mankind (without necessarily making God and man equal partners in the process of salvation).

This possibility of cooperation in the work of redemption is just one more example of the way God deals with his creatures throughout the history of salvation, giving them responsibility and participation in this saving work. This requires of mankind a form of community in which man can freely receive and accept God's promise of salvation and, under grace, realize it fully. This community, designed for the intensive and extensive growth of the work of salvation in the world, is the Church.

Here is revealed the ultimate meaning of the introduction of the interim period in the founding of the Church. It has not a proper purpose peculiar to itself. It exists as the pre-form and vital cell of the kingdom of God, which is to be brought to its full perfection through the cooperation of man with God's saving will. Through the Church and this interim period, objective redemption is to be brought to full perfection: all redeemed creatures are to gather before God in their free decision, thus giving perfect expression to the rule of God over all creation.

This is why the time of the Church is described as the time of the gathering together of the people of God (Matt. 28:19) or, what is the same thing, the age of mission (Rom. 15:16–24), of the call of the gentiles and of the encounter with the ungodly world.[22] This vocation of progressively revealing and fully realizing the hidden hegemony of God in this world makes it necessary for the Church to grow with history in time and place, to receive the riches of the nations and the great variety of all created existence into the realm of the redemption. All this is simply what the term "kingdom" means.

If this is so—the hidden coming of the *eschaton* in Christ and its gradual perfect revelation in history—then there must also be room left for the opposing powers to play their part in this history. It is also conceivable that these powers, realizing that their total and irrevocable annihilation is nearing, would raise themselves up in a last desperate counterattack. The Church's encounter with these powers is by no means an absolute evil, as if the Church would possibly be smothered or throttled by them. Rather, this conflict should be seen as God's chosen way of proving the power and vitality of the kingdom, whose growth is to take place precisely through such a victory. Such a plan corresponds to the Christ-event. For the diffusion of this event through the Church, whose head is Christ, can be accomplished only in the sign of the cross and death of the Lord, which must be imitated in the history of God's kingdom on earth just as much as the victory and resurrection.

The meaning of the interim time can also be understood from a different point of view: from the situation of the human individual and the conditions of his salvation. This approach is justified since the community accomplishes its salvation in the decision of the individual. Hence, the temporal extension of the end-phase will take the nature of the individual man into account and will be determined by it.

Here the concept of historicity must be recalled. "Being historical" is that fundamental component of human existence which requires man to realize and actualize his essence, which he does not possess completely and perfectly in a "now" of existence in time and, indeed, in accepting all the givens which his past and the world impose upon him. This means man is always open to the future, that he is always underway to that which he should be. Man enters the future by his free decision, in which he makes his encounter with the givens of his world and thereby comes to himself, his self-actualization and self-realization.

If God has established a supernatural goal for the fulfilment of human existence, then it is also understandable that he would offer this good to man both as something that has *already happened* (founding and providing the basis for his supernatural existence) as well as something that is yet to happen in the future. The actual order of salvation in which man actually exists corresponds to this presentation: in the free and responsible assumption of the salvation which appeared in Christ, man is to interiorize redemption within himself, further his own perfection thereby, and actualize and realize himself in a supernatural sense (of course, by virtue of grace).

Thus is man stretched out between the past and the future even with respect to salvation; he is in both possession and expectation. In this way, however, he is not simply given over to an event but is, rather, through his personal decision, a co-agent and coperformer.

To the essence of human historicity belongs not only position in time but also dependence on the community. Hence it is clear that the individual can accomplish his natural-supernatural fulfilment and self-realization only in communication with other men of both the past and the present. In all these points the suitability of the interim period and of the designation of Christ as the beginning and end of salvation-history for the needs of the individual man is revealed. This is another proof that individual and universal eschatology are closely connected with one another.

IV. THE PAROUSIA OF CHRIST AS THE FULL REVELATION OF THE LORDSHIP OF THE GOD-MAN IN HUMANITY AND THE COSMOS

The first coming of Christ was the founding end-event, whose powers are held and restrained during the interim time in a mysterious and hidden development. Consequently the parousia can be conceived of only as the full release of all these powers (with the corresponding complete destruction of all the opposing powers) and the full revelation of the glorified God-man in mankind and the cosmos.

The designation of this event as a revelation could cause the impression that there is a question here only of the publication of some reality already long existent but only hidden, and that now man actually sees it and learns about it. Such an understanding would run the risk of reducing the parousia of Christ to a mere external demonstration or public display of the power of the redeemer. The theory corresponding to this impression sees the decisive element in the whole event as a merely external, forensic judicial process.

In reality, however, revelation is an act of God in which God shares his life and grace with the world and mankind so that both are really affected and changed. This is also true of the eschatologically founded revelation in Jesus Christ, not only bringing the world new knowledge and understanding, not only even bringing the forgiveness of sins—understood merely morally—but also, in an incipient and hidden way, bringing divine life into the world and transforming it. These characteristics of event and deed must also be found in the complete eschatological revelation. This final revelation must, then, in consequence of its essential relationship to the historical Christ-event, visibly proclaim the salvation-power of Christ's death and resurrection in perfect measure and thus free all their effects to flood over mankind and the cosmos.

The relationship of the full revelation to the Christ-event of history can be seen even more closely—and in such a way that the individual elements of the parousia can be explained according to the Christ-revelation and its own proper nature. This is important for the interpretation of the mysterious manner of the second coming itself. The Christ-event and its presence in the Church make it impossible to regard this "coming" of the *kyrios* as a descent into a

Christ-less world and humanity, for Christ is indeed already present in the Church, even if in a signifying and sacramental way. There can be a question only of a new manner of his being present: Christ will finally remove the veils of his sacramental presence in the Church and make his theanthropic splendor so shine forth from the Church that the whole world will then be able to perceive it.[23]

Such a presentation of the second coming of Christ has two advantages. First, it overcomes the crude and merely cosmological presentation of this event. And second, it takes into account the meaning of the Church for the last event. It then becomes clear that the full revelation of the God-man will also be a transfiguration for the Church—which will emerge from its sacramental mode of existence and present itself in full clarity and reality as the *Christus totus,* the whole Christ, in the unity of her head and members.

The falling away of the veils will free Christ from the role of servant in which he has appeared to the world during the interim time; then he will appear in his own proper glory and lordship. This glorious lordship will extend itself in his full hegemony over mankind, which is really-symbolically represented in him. It will be the extension of the divine life, obtained in the redemptive work of Christ, from this same glorified Christ to all men; they will all be incorporated then into his body and fashioned to his transfiguration. In this way the full revelation of the lordship of Christ will effect the revitalization of that part of man which the effects of sin have cast into the prison of death—the resurrection of the flesh. The power of the Lord, no longer hemmed in by any bonds, will remove the fetters of death and at the same time give man a share in the immortal existence of his own body.

Such a participation in the eternal existence of the Lord will require, of course, that the manner of life of the resurrected body also conform to the manner of the glorified Christ's bodily existence. St. Paul speaks of this in the epistle to the Philippians when he alludes to the conformity of our body to the glorified body of Christ

(Phil. 3:21). The resurrection also means the transfiguration of the body into a new mode of existence, no longer subject to suffering and death, to injury and enfeeblement, and free from all the encumbrances of temporal, terrestrial existence. Only in this event of salvation will the perfect redemption of the body be accomplished. And likewise only with this event will the whole reality of man be elevated to perfection and full community with "the first born of the dead" (Col. 1:18).

As a consequence of the indissoluble union of the human body with the material cosmos, such a transformation must also affect all of the extrahuman creation, "according to the power he [Christ] has to subject all things to himself" (Phil 3:21). The community of destiny and existence between man and the cosmos will receive here its final confirmation. The glorification of the resurrected body will become the transfiguration of the whole material world, as the event of the new creation, according to the promise from the very beginning (Acts 3:21; 2 Pet. 3:13).

This also means that the cosmic cataclysms on the last day are not to be understood as bringing about the destruction of the material world. "The present state of this world will pass away" (1 Cor. 7:31), but only to make room for a new form of material existence, which will be a fitting "place" for the glorified life of the redeemed. The transition from the old form of existence to the new, supra-terrestrial and supra-temporal existence of the cosmos will involve a break, a revolution—this is the meaning of the apocalyptical images in the parousia statements. But it will also preserve continuity with the first creation, for God cannot disavow his first work. This process will reveal the high dignity of matter, that it is not at all to be regarded as the adversary of spirit and grace.

The attempt to understand this thoroughly mysterious change in the condition of the material world brings man face-to-face with several severe enigmas. This is especially so because man's present encounter with matter so impresses him with its obduracy and hostility that he cannot imagine it in any other way. However, here one must recall the admonition about the inadequacy of sense knowledge when dealing with transcendental reality. Sense perception cannot accompany the transition and maturation of the terrestrial-temporal into the transcendental-supra-temporal.

Like its divinely appointed beginning, the end of the material world will not really be a point in the line of time itself. The end will be rather the abrogation of the temporal and the historical; hence it cannot be interpreted in historical and cosmological categories. It is possible, however, to *think* meaningfully about this condition, for the fundamental relation between spirit and matter is not wholly imperceptible to the intelligence of man.

Both the natural sciences and anthropology show that matter is directed to and toward the spirit. Matter is the means whereby the spirit can express itself in a different medium.[24] The spirit's experience and encounter with the "other" enable it to become itself in a higher degree and manner. God himself uses matter in both creation and redemption in its function as sign for the spiritual and divine. This is quite evident in the integral nature of paradisiac man, whose material body was the perfect expression of his spirit and grace. This sign-fulness of matter is also used in the incarnation and, further, also in the realm of the sacramental.[25]

These considerations show that matter can be the expression and symbolization of spirit in more than one way or form. The history of creation and redemption shows an intensification of the symbolic power of matter, with a consequently greater penetration by the spirit, until the high point is reached in the resurrected body of Christ. Hence it is not unreasonable for the believer to think of the condition of the material world, after its break-through into the supra-temporal, in terms of the greatest possible spiritual penetration. In this state, matter will be so fully imbued with the spirit's own meaning and structure that it will lose its obduracy, its hostility, and become a completely pliable instrument of the spirit. It will receive the spirit's slightest impulses and become fully transparent to it.

This theological interpretation of matter can also be supported by the philosophy of nature. Modern scientific thought suggests a distinction between matter and corporality, contrasting the mass-quantitativeness of matter with a higher decorporalized condition, in which the characteristics of mass mellow into a qualitatively constituted unity. This concept so debilitates the law of extension and duration that a certain independence from merely external spatio-temporal conditions arises, making possible a conceptualization of the perfect state of matter as a pure expression of spirit.[26]

Although these remarks may not completely clarify the mysterious form of existence of the new material world, they do make it quite clear that the bodily transfiguration of man cannot be isolated from the transformation of all creation. For mankind, this transformation of the world means a new intensification of his corporeal-spiritual perfection as well as his supernatural happiness. Human nature, bound up with the whole cosmos—which on the one hand constitutes the place of man's self-realization, and for which, on the other hand, man himself constitutes the destiny—cannot reach its highest perfection without the cosmos.

All the dimensions of human reality can be considered to have entered full perfection only after the material world, the area of man's self-actualization, has been fully caught up and transformed by redeeming grace. The special state of happiness which this event will bring to man will be in this: that he will only then realize the meaning of his hegemony in creation. Matter will then be completely tractable to him, and he will see his longing for the universe fulfilled in the experience of the immeasurable richness of creation and his union with it.

This fulfilment cannot be accomplished in such a way that man would "be alone" with creation. The deepest impression of man will be the recognition of the mystery of conformity in Christ of the transformation of the cosmos, of the new material world and all individual things. This will be the experience of a new impulse toward Christ. For the whole purpose and goal of the transformation are not a simple "spiritualization" of matter (which would still be only a mere natural phenomenon), but its transfiguration to full and evident conformity to Christ. It is only in this state that man will really and fully grasp the mystery of creation in Christ (which is at the same time the mystery of the trinitarian structure of things) and the meaning of things in their ordination to Christ.

The dramatic event of the "Day of Christ" is a complex process, which we usually articulate into several acts (parousia, resurrection, judgment, transformation of the world), although the exact sequential arrangement of these acts has never been fully agreed upon. More important than the division into various acts is the unity of the whole drama and the functional unity of the individual elements; this is, of course, not to deny that such distinctions can be made.

The point of unity is the coming of Christ in glory. The dynamism of this event exerts itself in the resurrection of the dead, the perfection of the world and in the judgment—all together and at once—with the result that these "acts" cannot be separated from one another. The illegitimacy of such a separation is immediately evinced by the fact that the resurrection of the flesh causes new pain and suffering on the part of the damned. The judgment itself is accomplished in this "act." And there is likewise revealed in this one event the nature of the second coming of Christ as nothing other than the consummating revelation of his first coming—and the decision that this first coming calls into existence. For it is grace and judgment, redemption and rejection at one and the same time. The belief that it is Christ himself who will judge corresponds to this presentation (John 5:22; 2 Cor. 5:10; Rom. 2:10).

The fact that the judgment, resurrection and transformation of the world form an inner unity in the second coming of Christ does not mean that the judgment does not have a proper meaning and efficaciousness. This is especially true with respect to the individual judgment, which is not to be eliminated.[27] Such an individual judgment means that the general judgment at the end of time can be levied only on mankind as such: it is the judgment of the human race. This is the significance of the images used by the Bible to depict the universal and public character of this judgment. A public and general act of judgment is necessary at the end of time because mankind as a whole (with the Church as the innermost circle) has received the duty of coperforming the completion of redemption in history and of bringing about the unfolding of the Christevent. Christ will pass judgment on the degree of the accomplishment and nonaccomplishment of this communal task of humanity; hence in the universal judgment the entire achievement of world history will be included.

This judgment will not take place in the form of an external declaration that affixes itself to mankind from without. The revelation of Christ as truth and justice will affect man so deeply that he will see the worth or worthlessness of all historical activity reflected in Christ as in a mirror. And he will immediately experience in this reflection the judgment as grace or rejection, as entrance into Christ's glory or final and definitive exile. In this moment man will understand the mystery of all his history and the meaning of mankind's development with its high and low points. The historical meaning of the individual's own life will also be revealed, along with the historical effects of his good and bad acts.

This publication and illumination of man's unknown deeds and omissions in their engagement with universal history will not cause the redeemed shame and embarrassment. Its effect will be, on the contrary, to bring them to a full and definitive knowledge of the Christly dimension and mystery of history. Only in this knowledge, and in the act of revelation corresponding to it of the grace-judgment, will man see himself as the full and consummate reflection of historical existence.

The general judgment can effectively provide this fulfilment of human history, because it simultaneously effects the destruction of the demonic powers which have raged throughout history. The definitive defeat of satanic power will reveal to those who withstood its temptations, who remained faithful and true, the confessors and martyrs, the meaning of their suffering. And it will explain the abysmal mystery of evil in such a way that the supremacy of the redeeming grace of God will raise them up to their beatitude.

The inclusion of mankind in Christ's hegemony with the consequent exclusion of the evil from it, accomplished through the judgment, is the condition on which Christ can present creation, perfected in himself, to his heavenly Father (1 Cor. 15:24). In this act the kingdom of Christ matures into the perfect kingdom of God, and creation is elevated to full participation in the triune life of God.

The purpose of a believer's reflection on the fulfilment and consummation of mankind and the cosmos through and in Christ is not some sort of an apocalyptical revelation of future things and events. Christian eschatology belongs to the present "here and now" proclamation of salvation and to the present "here and now" realization and actualization of this present salvation. It is understood properly and correctly only if the Christian understands that he himself and the world are already now caught up in this transformation by Christ, and only if he then adapts his attitude and relationship to himself, mankind and the world accordingly.

NOTES

[1] Hence, M. Schmaus is correct when he says that eschatology is "developed Christology." *Kath. Dogmatik IV.* 2 (Munich: 1959), p. 219. Cf. also H. Urs v. Balthasar, "Eschatalogie," in: *Fragen der Theol-*

ogie heute, edited by Feiner-Trütsch-Böckle (Einsiedeln: 1957), p. 409. (Eng. tr. in preparation; Milwaukee.)

² For a fuller treatment of the idea of the new creation in the Old Testament, cf. G. Schneider, *Neuschöpfung oder Wiederkehr? Eine Untersuchung zum Geschichtsbild der Bibel* (Düsseldorf: 1961), pp. 15-34.

³ Cf. G. Lindesdog, *Studium zum neutestamentlichen Schöpfungsgedanken*, Acta Universitatis Upsaliensis II (Uppsala–Wiesbaden: 1952), p. 52.

⁴ Further justification from the O.T. could be found in the Royal Psalms (Ps. 47, 93, 96, 97, 99, etc.), in the Apocalypse of Isaiah (Is. 24–27), in the visions of Ezechiel (Ez. 36–39) and in Deutero-Zachary and Daniel.

⁵ Especially powerful descriptions of the figure and work of the Messiah can be found in Isaiah (7:14 ff.; 9:6 ff.; 11:1–10), Micheas (5:1 ff.), Ezechiel (34:23 f.) and Deutero-Isaiah (Is. 49:5; 53:2–12).

⁶ O. Cullmann, *Die Christologie des N.T.* (Tübingen: 1957), p. 143. (Eng. tr.: *Christology of the New Testament* [London: 1963].)

⁷ The question which arises here, whether Israel understood the messianic kingdom as an historical-earthly reality or as a new and transcendent aeon, cannot be treated in detail. Let it suffice to point out that the differences between the older prophecy and the later apocalyptical one need not be interpreted as contradictory.

⁸ Whether Jesus himself used this title as a designation for himself (and in which sense) is still disputed. The strongest denial is made by R. Bultmann in *Theologie des N.T.* (Tübingen: 1958), pp. 27, 31 f. (Eng. tr.: *Theology of the New Testament* [London].) However this opinion, which raises more problems than it solves (cf. O. Cullmann, *op. cit.*, p. 159), has also been rejected by Evangelical theologians. Cf. also W. Marxsen, *Anfangsprobleme der Christologie* (Gütersloh: 1960), pp. 20–34.

⁹ For a fuller examination of these parallels, cf. M. Barth, *Der Augenzeuge* (Zurich: 1946), pp. 128 f., and H. Berkhof, *Der Sinn der Geschichte: Christus* (Göttingen and Zurich: 1962), pp. 70 ff.

¹⁰ C. H. Dodd, *The Parables of the Kingdom* (London: 1935).

¹¹ This formulation of the theory comes from A. Schweitzer in his book, *Geschichte der Leben-Jesu-Forschung* (Tübingen: 1913), pp.

390–443. (Eng. tr.: *The Quest of the Historical Jesus* [London: 1954].) The theory has recently found a formidable defender in Martin Werner, *Die Entstehung des christlichen Dogmas* (2nd ed.; Bern-Tübingen: 1953). Consequent eschatology maintains that Jesus predicted the definitive end of the world for the generation living at that time and wished to prepare it through his death as a messianic sign. Naturally, then, this theory must also take into account a major error on the part of Jesus.

[12] Compare the following statements about the Son of Man in Matthew 24:27; Mark 8:38; 14:62; Luke 17:26 ff. with Mark 2:10; 8:31; 10:45.

[13] Cf. R. Schnackenburg, *God's Rule and Kingdom* (New York: 1963), pp. 195–214.

[14] For a discussion of the not-so-easy question whether these pictures are realistic or merely spiritualistic, cf. H. M. Biedermann, *Die Erlösung der Schöpfung beim Apostel Paulus* (Würzburg: 1940), pp. 34 ff.

[15] Cf. G. Schneider, *op. cit.*, p. 69.

[16] H. Biedermann, *op. cit.*, pp. 54 f.

[17] One cannot maintain that the Synoptics' view of the eschatological cosmic events was that of a formal annihilation of the world on the basis of such texts as Matthew 24:35; Mark 13:31, and Luke 21:33.

[18] Cf. G. Schneider, *op. cit.*, p. 73.

[19] Cf. also F. Malmberg, *Ein Leib—ein Geist. Vom Mysterium der Kirche* (Freiburg: 1960), pp. 258 f.

[20] "Man is called a little cosmos, not because he is composed of the four elements (for every living nature, even the most insignificant, is likewise composed), but because he possesses all the powers of the cosmos. For in the cosmos are gods, the four elements, as well as non-rational animals and plants. And man has all these powers. For as spiritual power he has the logical; he also has the nature of the elements, the nourishing, the growing and the reproducing of the same kind." ("Library" of Photius.) Cf. also W. Kranz, *Kosmos* (Bonn: 1958), p. 105.

[21] Cf. Cyrill v. Korvin-Krasinski, "Engel—Mensch—Kosmos," in: *Liturgie und Mönchtum*, Laacher Hefte 21 (Maria-Laach: 1957), pp. 91–109.

[22] Cf. R. Schnackenburg, *op. cit.*, pp. 193 ff.

[23] A. Winklhofer, *Das Kommen seines Reiches* (Frankfort: 1959), p. 191.

[24] Cf. K. Rahner, "Die Christologie innerhalb einer evolutiven Weltanschauung," in: *Schriften zur Theologie V* (Einsiedeln: 1962), pp. 191 f. (Eng. tr.: *Theological Investigations V* [Baltimore: Helicon, 1965].)

[25] Cf. L. Scheffczyk, "Die materielle Welt im Lichte der Eucharistie," in: *Aktuelle Fragen zur Eucharistie*, ed. M. Schmaus (Munich: 1960), pp. 156–79.

[26] For a fuller treatment, cf. H. E. Hengstenburg, *Der Leib und die letzten Dinge* (2nd ed.; Regensburg: 1955).

[27] Nevertheless, the relationship between the individual and the general judgment is not to be understood objectively and temporally as a prior and posterior serialization.

PART THREE

The Christian Lives in the World

Consecratio Mundi

by M.-D. Chenu, O.P.

Consecratio mundi—not too long ago this phrase seemed quite commonplace in the current vocabulary and, if one may use the expression, more "pietistic" than formally meaningful. Today, however, it takes on a definite meaning in technical richness and in ecclesial significance: a fortunate result of the Church's renewed awareness of herself as the Christian community involved in the world. This, in turn, is a reaction against the break between the Church and civil society which has occurred for a great number of reasons.

Consequently, the phrase draws its original power from the fact that it refers to the role of the laity in the building-up of the Church, its role in the "presence" of the Church within the world. As testimony in its favor, it will be sufficient to cite one notable text which, without having full magisterial solemnity, is nevertheless supported by it by the highest authority. During the Second World Congress of the Lay Apostolate (held in Rome, October 5–13, 1957), Pope Pius XII proclaimed the work of the faithful layman to its full extent:

> Aside from the small number of priests, the relations between the Church and the world require the intervention of lay apostles. The *consecratio mundi* is essentially the work of the laymen themselves, of men who are intimately a part of economic and social life and who participate in the government and in legislative assemblies.[1]

In its wording, in its doctrine and context, no statement confirms this better than what the then Cardinal Montini wrote several years later in his pastoral letter of 1962 to the Church of Milan:

> ... This is why she [the Church] will call upon the laity, her good and faithful lay Catholics, to form a link between her supernatural domain, wholly devoted to religion, and the temporal domain of society in which they live. By a sort of delegation, she will confide to their docile and skilled collaboration the difficult and very beautiful task of the *consecratio mundi,* that is [note carefully the words used], to permeate the vast realm of the profane world with Christian principles and powerful natural and supernatural virtues.[2]

Yet within the large body of writing which uses this expression to define the object and the end of the lay apostolate, one cannot fail to observe a certain wavering usage; its meaning is sometimes expanded, sometimes restricted, sometimes taken as rigorously conceptual, sometimes surrendered to oratorical exhortation.[3] In view of this instability of usage, it is not inopportune to analyze both the precise conceptual content of the phrase and the supple connotations which, in its periphery of ideas, bring out the delicate interplay of complementary truths.

For it is one of the laws of language—and theological language must observe these laws—that words and spoken sounds are not rigid, inflexible units, but call for an aura of radiations and fringes around an essential semantic nucleus; although they are quite indeterminate, these fringes are extremely useful for an understanding of the realities which they signify. To put it into a formula: words have a precise, specific meaning about a content determined by a "formal object" and an order of specific causes; they also have a generic meaning, corresponding to the signified reality's zone of influence, according to its connections with adjoining realities. As the logician would say, the specific meaning is limited in extension to the same degree that it is determined in comprehension, while the general meaning is proportionately more extended as it remains indeterminate in comprehension.

For example, the word "society" can be taken in the very general sense of any grouping, however little it may be organized; but it can also be taken in the precise sense of a definite group established by a contract, subject to an authority, having an administrative body and a government, for the purpose of defending interests, and so on—that by which it is distinguished from a different group, called a community, whose constitutive characteristics are different.

Both meanings of the word are legitimate and even necessary for a fruitful understanding. It would be a mistake to discard the use of a general sense on the pretext of strictness of expression and technical precision; but it would also be a mistake to disregard the findings of an analysis which has defined the semantic nucleus and has established the "formal" concept of a reality.

All this applies also to *consecratio mundi* as it is accepted in today's terminology. From a theological, spiritual and apostolic viewpoint, this is a favorable time to weigh the full force of the expression; it is particularly fitting to determine its precise, formal meaning, with full allowance for the truth and the effectiveness of its general meaning. It is this estimate which we shall attempt to establish here.

THE SCOPE OF THIS ANALYSIS OF MEANING

There is no question of yielding to scholastic subtlety to devise an abstract definition to be used among specialists. As the authorities quoted testify, the phrase itself expresses well the actual role of the faithful in the profane world, the land of God's kingdom, the scene of the incarnation of divine life among men. What is the real influence of man's activity in the world, carried on by a man who looks on the world in the light of his faith and is committed to its upbuilding through the resources of grace?

Here we find ourselves at a crossroads: on the one hand (through the growth of civilization as evidenced by a rapid evolution of the structures of mankind), the world is becoming vividly aware of the earthly values which it bears; meanwhile, on the other hand, the Christian community is searching for the impact of its faith on these profane values—values which are more and more emancipated from the close religious tutelage of the previous era. The desacralization of nature and of society seems to be a natural result of a scientific and technological civilization. Consequently, we are not going to define the role of the Christian layman through an abstract deduction from theoretical principles, but rather by an examination of the human material which he will have to take into account, first for his own benefit, then for the earthly well-being of his brothers, and finally for the concomitant upbuilding of God's kingdom.

In recalling the copious investigations conducted from every angle, both pastorally and doctrinally oriented, we are sure that one of the chapters in the theology of the relationship between nature and grace is being written today in the full life of the Church, in her apostolic activity and in her Christocentric teaching. The phrase *consecratio mundi*, however, certainly does not try to express the whole of this experience and this truth, but only one of its essential themes.

The coming of Vatican Council II has given a public, or, we might say, an institutional utterance to this problem. One of the chief topics on its agenda has been just that—to determine the relation of the laity within a Church which has come to understand that she is not a levitical, "clerical" society, but a community of believers structured through an apostolic hierarchy.[4]

"CONSECRATIO"

What is the precise meaning of *consecratio*? We are seeking to fix the meaning of a specific concept and, as we just pointed out, its comprehension as well; this will give us the occasion to indicate the limit of its extension to other connected, though marginal, realities.

Consecration is a process by which man, whether commissioned by an institution or not, withdraws something from common usage or draws a person away from his primary availability in order to set him apart for the divinity with the purpose of giving full homage to God's mastery over his creature. Thus, it is the abstraction of a reality from its own end, from that finality which is defined by the laws of its nature—the laws of its physical nature, its psychological make-up, its social involvement, or the free disposition of self, if we are speaking of a person endowed with freedom. It is an alienation in the best (or the worst) sense of the word, a transferral to him who is the highest sovereign, to the source of all being and to the end of all perfection.

After it has been set apart, the sacred object is untouchable, in an almost physical sense of the word; so much so, that a person will handle it only with approved gestures, with "rites" which manifest this seclusion. A sacred place must no longer be used for the ordinary needs of life, under pain of sacrilegious violation; no one enters it without surrounding himself, both exteriorly and interiorly, with the isolation of the gods. A sacred action—from the ancient anointing and coronation of kings (and even the protocol of today's heads of state) to the common, everyday burial of the dead—breaks, in its gestures and in its outcome, with the habitual conduct of social life, with its services as well as with its vulgarisms.

At least within the bounds of his consecration, a consecrated person must be separated in thought and feeling, in body and dress from the occupations, work, interests and behavior of other men. Social and religious historians attest to all of this, even in the most meaningful of corrupt practices (such as superstitious taboos), and in still more concrete terms than theologians in their classic definitions.

Evidently, this sacralization can have different levels, both in intensity and practical application; in fact, its limits are quite variable according to the times, the milieu and social customs. In short, consecration has its own depth; we can evaluate its original character if we compare it to a lesser action, which is a simple *blessing*. In a blessing, the object is certainly referred to the divinity, to whom it is offered or who takes it under his protection; but this object keeps its natural function, its earthly usage, its utilitarian ends. Blessed bread is respected, but also eaten.

The sacred appears in all its individuality if we compare it to the *holy*. The two concepts are certainly subject to constant confusion, and even to some justifiable synonymous usage. But the fact is that, formally, and without pushing the abstraction of this analysis too far, *holiness* has characteristics which differ from those of *sacredness*. God is "holy," the Holy par excellence; yet he is not specifically sacred. Holiness is the pre-eminent dignity within the very innermost self of the being, which is acquired by participation in divine life. Despite this close union with him who transcends, holiness does not relinquish its original state. During its beginning, its "initiation," and in its growth, it may require certain sacral means of operation and separation; yet these are merely the earthly conditions of a "grace" which, in contrast, seizes the being in the fullness of its real nature—in its profane nature, we might say. In becoming sacred, the profane ceases to be profane; in becoming holy, it remains profane.

A PROFANE WORLD

The profane confronts the sacred. A profane reality—object, act, person, group—is that which preserves in its existence, within its workings and in its ends, the basic stability of its nature. But if this reality is a being which is conscious of its activity and its purpose, then this consciousness of its activity and purpose is at once both the primary value and the rule of its perfection. Wheat gathered in the harvest, processed and marketed in the economic order for the nourishment of men, clearly remains a profane reality, even though those who harvested and processed it worked for the glory of God, toward their personal holiness, and in the service of their brothers.

When the agricultural engineer leaves for an underdeveloped country in order to organize the rich productiveness of its land for a better world according to modern techniques, through his charity he performs a work which is sanctifying to a high degree, both in personal grace and within the Christian community; yet his involvement in Catholic Action does not make him leave his profane calling, his "laicity," any more than it suspends him from economic laws in buying and selling. The same holds true for a nation which is clearly permeated by Christian values in its institutions and its legislation; it still remains a political society, autonomous in its field.

Persons and things, therefore, can be involved in the over-all movement toward a supernatural end and be fully affected by Christian virtues; their dedication to supernatural ends and Christian virtues does not diminish the objective content of their nature, nor does it dispense from its laws. To be a gift of God, wheat must nonetheless still be cultivated. Likewise, the nation which attains its common good, both naturally and supernaturally, does not become a theocratic society. *Gratia non tollit naturam, sed perficit.* Grace does not "sacralize" nature; in making it partake of divine life, it restores it to itself, so to speak.

The examples are not hastily chosen to illustrate an abstract thesis; they represent the characteristic activity of a new civilization. In such a civilization, through his scientific discovery of the forces of nature and through his technological control over his powers, man no longer feels so struck by the mystery of nature's powers, which formerly forced him to appeal to the awesome might of the divinity. Now that he is acquainted with them, as he uncovers their underlying causes and even lays hold of them in order to build a universe in which his spirit becomes flesh, man desacralizes nature by making a kingdom out of it for himself in an exalting act of sovereignty. Such is the new condition of man in a civilization of work, in which man molds nature into human form.

The individual and collective repercussions of such a revolutionary mode of thinking are somewhat disturbing to man's religious sensibility. Yet in itself this sacralization is natural; and if in the twentieth century it takes on a cosmic dimension, this is due to an over-all application to mankind as it becomes aware of its earthly destiny. This progressive awareness can be observed by anthropologists and ethnologists in earlier civilizations, all things being equal, as well as in the stages of Western Christian civilization itself.

Furthermore, and in order to thwart a certain panicky imagination in the face of what is called the atheism of an industrial civilization, let us firmly understand that to desacralize the world, to purge it of its gods and demons, lies within the deepest law of Christianity: "in making it an object of creation external to God, he released it for men and made experimental science and technology possible" (J. Lacroix). We can question whether the Hindu, Buddhist, and even Islamic religions will resist the spread of a scientific and industrial mentality; but Christianity can give its straightforward consent, since it is the Word of God addressed to men, and not an outgrowth of a referral (*re-ligio*) of nature to God.

Faith is of a different order than "religion"; and if it can become psychologically, morally, cultually firm only through certain religious acts, at least by giving religion its proper place, it keeps itself untainted by a heaviness harmful to its gratuitous character. "True science," as Paul VI said, "has demystified, desacralized the phenomena of nature; it has contributed to purifying the faith of its slag, of certain superstitions, and of a certain dread or insecurity complex."[5]

A "MISSIONARY" CHURCH

Here we come to the profound reason for the new relationship between the Church and the world which is beginning in this day—a reason at once institutional and evangelical, the strategic and doctrinal focal point of all the problems which have gripped the Christian consciousness and which find expression at the highest level in Vatican Council II. *Ecclesia ad intra, Ecclesia ad extra:* beneath this balanced formula lies an incisive program,[6] oriented not toward two juxtaposed problems but toward a single issue—what must the Church be, in herself, to bear witness to the Word of God in the world, in the new world of the twentieth century? This is no longer merely the question of the relationship between science and faith, as at Vatican I, nor only the question of harmony between Church and State. It is an even more radical issue—the relationship between civilization (the building of this world) and evangelization.

As a result of progress which is ambiguous but good in itself, the foremost characteristic of this new world is the direct acceptance of responsibility for the common needs of mankind by diverse economic and political communities. Such is the happy result of socialization, as John XXIII understood it. Henceforth, the essential components of all human society—physical subsistence, economic organization, organs of culture, care for the sick and the aged, reconstruction after natural disasters, and, beyond all this, a striving toward social justice, toward a peace in brotherly solidarity among men which reaches beyond race and continent—all those things which, until today, have been more or less directly inspired and directed by the Church in the West for more than a thousand years, have become the common good of all mankind itself, the object of its highest hopes. Likewise, man becomes conscious of the laws of *his* nature insofar as he discovers and uses the laws of *all* nature. The world *exists*. Yet this does not make it less liable to "contempt."

The autonomy of the world from the Church does not imply an absolute independence; however, it does go beyond the realm of mere empirical concessions and practical opportunism. The good ordering of terrestrial reality, the common good of human groups on all levels (family, corporation, nation, humanity itself), possesses value as an end, a secondary one and beneath the final end, but an *end* and not just a means. Within this integrated ordering of human values, the transition from sacred to profane is not the collapse feared by Augustine's theology, for whom the profane was merely a world to be made holy.

The historic arrival of this autonomy shows that if in the course of history the Church has eminently filled high social functions (aid to the poor, care for the sick, collective security, popular education, peace), she did so through a *substitution* for the ineffectiveness of human groups which were inadequately organized. Today, in a universe which is consciously building itself, we leave behind us a "Christendom," that is, a Church endowed with specifically earthly powers merged with her real powers received from Christ and used temporally to spread the gospel. The sacralization of institutions and ways of life was the means for collective and personal sanctification; on occasion it even substituted for evangelization.

The Church of the twentieth century no longer has to take upon herself the ordering of civilization or the building of nations; rather, she must spread evangelical leaven among these civilizations, within the structures of mankind. It is not the business of the Church to nourish mankind, to oversee economic projects, to provide measures of security, to undertake agrarian reforms, to establish a level of culture in underdeveloped countries. But she must collectively pledge her faith, her hope, and her charity, her "political charity" (Pius XI) to serve the upbuilding of a fraternal humanity. Her task is not to construct a "Christian world" at her own expense and on her own initiative, but to Christianize the world exactly as it is being built. In a way, the Church must go out of herself; she must be *missionary*.

For this very same reason, the involvement of the laity in the building of God's kingdom is in no way whatever a subsidiary function, a complementary role in the service of the clergy, the ones entitled to the task; theirs is a constitutive role within the realm of true evangelical responsibility, where obedience in doctrine and discipline does not dilute the quality or the truthfulness of the engagement. The involvement in *profane* organization is precisely what makes the function of the laity within the ecclesial body essential to the spread of the gospel. Neither theocratic imperialism, nor premature sacralization, nor clerical mandate replaces the universal rule of the grace of Christ.

THE COSMIC DIMENSION OF THE INCARNATION

But then, how is this universal rule of God to become effective over all human reality? How else, if not through a "setting apart" for God, as in the natural religions?

The incarnation of Christ is developed and fulfilled in an incorporation in which all reality, including every human value, enters into his body, and in which all creation will be "consummated." "For the universe itself (and not merely mankind) is to be freed from the shackles of mortality and enter upon the liberty and splendor of the children of God" (Rom. 8:17–23). For the Logos incarnate, the redeemer, fulfilled the work of the Logos creator: the identity of the Person does not allow the work of redemption to be severed from the work of creation; this identity gives cosmic scope to the incarnation, in which all creation finds its unity. The Church, Christ's body, cannot be considered as a pure and simple "case apart" within creation any more than the hypostatic union, just as creation cannot be considered alone, as achieved and complete in itself from the viewpoint of theology, without recourse to the incarnation.[7]

In a manner of speaking, there is nothing "profane" about a Christian any more ("All is in us, we are in Christ"); the distinction between the profane and the sacred has dissolved. But by eliminating this distinction, we no longer show sufficiently the individual depth of every created being which comes from the Word creator under the sanctifying assumption of the flesh by the Word incarnate and redeemer. Thus in Christ, the personal identity of the Word, creator and incarnate, does not decrease the autonomy of his human activity under the ruling Word. Monophysitism is not merely the heresy of some bad teachers; it is the bent of an "idealism" which thinks of the profane only as material for the holy.

In using the broad sense of the word *consecration* too freely, we once again risk falling unwittingly into theocratic and clerical usages (the word can never be transferred to mean sacralization itself). Even a certain devotion to Christ the King is not free from such an unfortunate time-lag, a devotion nearer to the regulations and requirements of the Old Covenant than to the gospel. The same would hold for a type of spirituality centered on Christ the High Priest, if the sacral categories should overemphasize it; whereas the epistle to the Hebrews uses these categories only to bring to mind a Priesthood whose reality transcends all rites and in the end gives them their true meaning.

THE TIMELINESS OF A VOCABULARY

In brief, the problem at hand is one of using cultual categories to express the Christian mystery and to make it relevant.

First of all, such a usage is clearly essential, from the very fact that worship is needed in which faith in the mystery finds outward expression, adapted to the human condition and to the specifically "religious" requirements of an encounter with the God of faith. Consequently, if union with God in Christ is basically a movement of the *theologal* life which enlivens man's whole existence, then it remains that faith, hope and charity are also nourished within worship in which the *moral* virtue of "religion," in regulating the relationship with the divinity, rules once again in full power.[8]

What is more, an external and tangible worship is within the very logic of the incarnation, whose mystery continues in fact and is expressed in the sacraments; from baptism, or incorporation in Christ, to the Eucharist, the earthly fulfilment of the mystery, these take the form of "consecrations." It is here that we must recognize a properly Christian meaning, within the word itself, which to a great degree exceeds the restricted sense which we would be tempted to reserve for it were we to forget the true nature of the sacraments. Actually, these sacraments have meaning only in relation to a reality—*res sacramenti*—which is that of life itself in Christ, gathering the universe unto the glory of the Father and restoring all the values of primordial creation.

Finally, the cultual vocabulary has been spiritualized, deritualized, according to the explicit current of thought in the New Covenant ("worship in the spirit" in St. John; the epistle to the Hebrews). The use of the word *consecration* has spread beyond the various forms of "separation," of "setting apart," which the sacramental order itself recognizes. Henceforth, it is the normal thing to use cultual categories for presenting sanctifying and sanctified realities, in thought as well as in speech. This is what justifies, to a certain degree, the use of the word *consecration* to designate an aspect of the sanctification of the profane through the grace of Christ.

The expression *consecratio mundi* is likewise valid and beneficial. But to use it well, and in a valid way, is possible only after an immediate and necessary adjustment, by placing it correctly within an entire framework whose good balance, both in doctrine and in practice, ensures the most refined truth. Indeed, the great size of each room within this structure of the economy of the incarnation very readily involves an overemphasis, a gain which conceals other essential elements for a greater or lesser interval of time. Through much hard work, we have been able to recognize this in the consequences of Counter-Reformation theology.

Moreover, for several centuries, beginning with a Christendom in which the sociological sacralization of the civil order and of human values served as an earthly support for the expression of the Christian mystery, we have belittled both in doctrine and in practice the specific truthfulness of natural realities and secondary causes, the object of "profane" sciences. The building of the world, and, for example, each man's professional work, were no more than the occasion, the intentional matter, for the sanctification of the Christian in the world, the dull locale of a provisional existence. Whence the simply negative role of the faithful layman, busy with his own toil.

Today, through a new awareness which is recorded at the highest point in the Council and may even characterize it, the Church rediscovers her relationship to the world *as such,* within nature and within history. At the same time, she returns to the lay Christian his place in the very constitution of the Church, not by a masked clericalization, nor by his chance involvement in Christian institutions, but by his very being, by partaking in the mystery through the virtues of faith, hope and charity: theologal life, beyond all cultual "religion." All his works, in knowledge and in action, are sanctified;

they become "holy" in Christ the consummator, without necessarily being sacralized or clerically institutionalized. The universe is permeated, invaded by grace, without being set apart from its natural destiny. Consecration of the world means the sanctification of men.

True, all reality is taken up within this sanctifying grace, which is individual and collective (within the Church); all reality is swept on by the supreme end, recapitulation in Christ, far beyond what it has by nature and its temporal destiny. True. But this eschatological finality does not reduce secondary causes to mere means, the makeshift scaffolding of a heavenly dwelling. Profane activities, and especially science, economics and politics, lose none of their own vigor beneath the imperative of the final end which will fulfil them. The order of created things remains under the control of their own ends within that order, according to the creative plan, although they are subordinated ends. Hope does not become alien to the world.

Let us say, then, that *formally* speaking the expressions "construction of the world" and "consecration of the world" have contrary implications.[9] By definition, the Christian layman involved in the world does not consider himself or his works as "set apart." Of course, as a son of God, he is certainly not "of the world"; but the lofty spirituality of the *exile,* of *contempt for the world,* of man the *pilgrim,* is true only within the core of the whole Christian mystery—the mystery of a recapitulation of all truth and all goodness by Christ, in whom creation once again finds its unity.

Therefore, if the theme of *consecratio mundi* carries a beneficial truth, if it is worth being put forth and discussed in its generic sense within current teaching, it would not seem timely to attribute to it the value of a doctrinal definition built up from the exact meaning of the word *consecration*. For then, in the present juncture of doctrinal and pastoral theology, there would be a serious danger of rendering ambiguous both the eventual positive definition of the layman and the exact determination of the relationship between the

Church and the world. When it comes to language, truth demands timeliness.

ADDENDUM

At the time this study was published (June, 1964), the Doctrinal Commission of Vatican Council II, in preparation for the third session, had just met and, after a discussion, approved by a very small majority the following text (*Constitutio de Ecclesia,* cap. 4, *De laicis,* n. 34 in fine): "Sic et laici, qua adoratores ubique sancte agentes, ipsum mundum Deo consecrant" ("In this way also the laity as worshippers acting everywhere in a holy manner consecrates to God the world itself").

The explanatory justification that accompanies the text submitted to the Council states: this is true "aliquo sensu," and should be understood in such a way that the "proper character of temporal things would be integrally preserved" ("Rerum temporalium indoles propria integre servari debet"). On the strength of this clarification, the text was adopted both by the Commission and by the Council. Yet this clarification, besides not appearing in the text itself, simply confirms the regrettable ambiguity of the phrase.

Formally speaking, a distinction should be made between *sanctificatio* (used to define exactly the role of the laity in the world; *ibid.,* n. 31: "fermenti instar ad mundi sanctificationem velut ab intra conferant" ["that they, like leaven, would contribute toward the sanctification of the world as it were from within"]), *oblatio* (cf. *ibid.,* n. 34: "Patri piisime offeruntur" ["they are offered most devoutly to the Father"]), and *consecratio.* The world is not "sacralized" but sanctified through the theologal life (comprised of the three theological virtues) of the faithful.

NOTES

[1] AAS 49 (1957), p. 427; NCWC translation: Washington, D.C., par. 19.

[2] *Osservatore Romano*, March 23, 1962.

[3] This is the case in the many commentaries which Pius XII's statement aroused. For example, see *Wort und Wahrheit* (October-November-December, 1958) on the nature and the requirements of a *consecratio mundi*; also, the articles of G. Lazzati, professor at the University of Milan: "La *consecratio mundi* essenzialmente opera dei laici," in: *Studium* (December, 1959); "L'apostolato dei laici oggi" in a special issue on the Catholic laity, *Orientamenti pastorali* (March, 1961), published under the auspices of Milan's Center of Pastoral Orientation.

[4] Cf. the monumental schema of Vatican Council II, as well as *De Ecclesia*, promulgated at the end of the third session. (Translator's note.)

[5] Interview with Cardinal Leger regarding the Council, quoted in the French newspaper *Le Monde* (July 18, 1963).

[6] Note that at the end of the first session of the Council, Cardinal Suenens defined in these very words the theme around which the material to be debated must center, although this was not brought out clearly in the preparatory schemata.

[7] Here we refer, sometimes even word for word, to P. B. Dupuy's analysis of the recent works of K. Rahner, A. Grillmeier and F. Malmberg on the mystery of the incarnation in connection with creation. *Revue des Sciences Philosophiques et Theologiques* (1963), pp. 106–110.

[8] Cf. St. Thomas, *In Boethium de Trinitate*, q. 3, a. 2: "Whether faith ought to be distinguished from religion."

[9] Contrary implications which have become manifest in the wording of texts at Vatican II; one of these texts described *consecratio mundi* as the task proper to the layman, and another (the famous Schema 17) spoke of "the presence of the Church in the world," a world desacralized according to the legitimate profane autonomy of the causes and standards of its construction.

The Christian's Responsibility for Freedom

by HEINZ ROBERT SCHLETTE

WHEN FREEDOM IS DISCUSSED today,[1] it can be done only when one considers those past and present realities which have nothing in common with freedom as such. Therefore we are not here concerned with giving a discourse in praise of freedom—as it were, a memorial to what men formerly called "freedom." It is only in meeting the lack of freedom that we can today significantly think, write, and speak about freedom, its nature, and its demands.

This situation, however, should not be understood as though thinking about freedom were possible only in the well-known political controversies. The real difficulty, more precisely, is to concern oneself much more positively and constructively with freedom in view of the many ghostly faces of "unfreedom." The real difficulty thus is to understand freedom not only from its opposite, the friend-enemy relationship, but from its own structure and significance. With this approach to the problem, the existential relevance of freedom becomes completely clear, and at the same time we avoid an overly narrow view. It is not easy for anyone to think and speak with detached impartiality and indifference about an issue in which he is most deeply involved. Since we are, however, convinced that the thinking of a man equipped with mind and freedom still keeps its legitimacy after such an involvement, we must adapt ourselves to the demands and ground rules of this thinking and begin with resolved objectivity.

If the methods and habits of thought have demanded our entire commitment, so also does the very topic to which we now turn: freedom, and more exactly, the responsibility which the Christian has for freedom. One must immediately ask whether man can be responsible for freedom at all. Is not freedom the kind of thing that we always "have"—such as free will, freedom of choice, and freedom of action, which traditional philosophy teaches? And is not it the kind of thing with which we have always acted? Perhaps, then, shouldn't "responsibility for freedom" be called only "correct use of freedom"? If responsibility for freedom were concerned only with its correct usage, then our topic would be in the general field of ethics, and we would have to emphasize that the free man has to conduct himself according to moral norms.

But Western thought has for a long time now concerned itself basically with something else: on the one hand, the norms according to which freedom is to be used have been brought into question; on the other, the concept and the issue of freedom are in no way still taken for granted and uncritically assumed, as happens in the average talk about the right use of freedom. In a more penetrating consideration of freedom, therefore, responsibility for freedom undoubtedly does not mean the correct use of freedom, but freedom itself.

With this first agreement it is true that we have avoided a possible misunderstanding, but new questions arise immediately: What is the freedom for which the Christian is responsible? And what kind of responsibility is this? As with all living, concrete acts in which one has his existence, so too in the case of freedom is it a waste of time to work on a "definition of the concept." Therefore we shall immediately turn to freedom itself; we shall proceed to describe it and, insofar as it is here possible, to take up questions we meet.

The freedom for which the Christian has to assume responsibility —a responsibility which, although it has not appeared today for the first time, nevertheless is of particular concern today—has in my opinion two forms: the freedom of which the New Testament speaks—we call this *eschatological freedom*—and the freedom of every human person in the order of the State, that is, social and political freedom, the freedom of thinking, working, believing and speaking, of science and of the press; I call this second form of freedom *secular freedom*. The expression "secular" (*welthaft*) is not the best; yet I do not want to call the freedom "worldly" (*weltlich*), because that could suggest the idea that we are dealing with a worldly and an unworldly or spiritual freedom, or with a natural and a supernatural freedom. In what follows we will try as much as possible to avoid such distinctions, which are loaded with philosophical and theological problems.[2]

Eschatological freedom signifies first of all—which might sound surprising—present freedom. It is present among us as the *basileia tou Theou*, the dominion and kingdom of God. The fullness of time has begun; the perfection of all things has become a reality. Jesus the Christ has been experienced as the first witness of the new creation by the community of those who have been called from the mass of the people and have become worthy to enter into that completely new form of existence which the New Testament calls *pistis*, faith. The faith of the New Testament, and therefore of the Christian, in its original and true meaning refers to the entrance of the *community* into union with the risen Messiah Jesus, whom every page of the New Testament calls the *Kyrios*, the Lord.

The only way man can enter this community is totally and without reserve. The old man is crucified with Christ (Rom. 6:6); he is laid aside like a garment (Col. 3:9; Eph. 4:22). The old has gone, and a completely new creation appears, a *kaine ktisis* (2 Cor. 5:17; Gal. 6:15), a newness of life (2 Cor. 5:17), and that means the fullness of time and existence (Gal. 4:4; Eph. 1:10). The new wine bursts the old skins (Mk. 2:22; Matt. 9:17; Lk. 5:37–39); the water of the old aeon is changed into the wine of the dominion of God (John 2:1–10). Those who have been invited and chosen, those who have been given a share in the faith of the new existence in Christ (which signifies love and unity), celebrate the eschatological banquet with God (Lk. 14:15–23). After John the Baptist had proclaimed the tidings that "the Messiah will come," the proclamation of Jesus is: "the time is fulfilled"—this by all means is the testimony of the gospels (cf. Mk. 1:1–15).

The presence of the kingdom of God is again and again characterized in the New Testament by the word "new." Even the liturgy, especially that of the central eschatological feast, Easter, announces the discovery of the *novitas*, the newness of existence, in contrast to the moribund *vetustas*, the aged and senile aeon. The newness of the existence which can be achieved in faith is both indicative and imperative. It signifies that something *has happened* to man, that he finds his end not at the side of man but at the side of God; at the same time it *requires* that the new existence entrusted to man be embraced by him and exercised in a life of assent, fidelity and hope. You *are* holy, we read time and again, and then follows the imperative: *live* in a way that is fitting for saints and citizens of the dominion of God.

The eschatological, new life in and from unity with Christ is proclaimed by John and Paul in continually new ideas and pictures. Exegesis and theology have long recognized that the experience of the resurrection of Jesus was the central event for the primitive community. Its members recognized this event as the initial transformation of the earth, as the basis for firm faith, and as the conquest of death and sin, the characteristics of the old aeon. The new life was described in human terms like peace, joy, hope, truth, fullness. It was conceived as "being in Christ" or "abiding in him." In fact it was understood simply as freedom.

The eschatological existence comprehended and realized in faith could be called freedom just as well as imitation; it could be described with the pictures of the wine and the meal just as well as with the sign of the washing of feet. All these statements and pictures refer to that great incomprehensible mystery which surpasses the possibilities of human language, that mystery of the kingdom of God which has become present on earth. Freedom must be called eschatological because it is a constituent of that new—of the already anticipating coming—form of existence which could be opened up only by God.

All this could be explained as fanaticism or gnosticism, if it were not for that decisively important "but." This difficulty endangers the authenticity of what has been presented up to now, but it is nevertheless a prime characteristic of the presence of the eschatological: the *eschata*, the last things, the dominion of God, are present, but only in the form of a mystery, which as such is still not revealed and manifest. Paul sketched this situation of our epoch in salvation-history with clear terms in the famous eighth chapter of his letter to the Romans (18–25):

> For I reckon that the sufferings of our present time are not worthy to be compared with the glory to come that will be revealed in us. For the eager longing of creation awaits the revelation of the sons of God. For creation was made subject to vanity (impermanence) . . . in hope, because creation itself also will be delivered from its slavery to corruption into the freedom of the glory of the sons of God. For we know that all creation groans and travails in pain until now.
>
> And not only it, but we ourselves also who have the first fruits of the Spirit—we ourselves groan within ourselves, waiting for the adoption as sons, the redemption of our body. For in hope were we saved. But hope that is seen is not hope. For how can a man hope for what he sees? But if we hope for what we do not see, we wait for it with patience.

Pauline and Johannine theology, indeed that of the entire New Testament, sees a striking conflict: the kingdom of God has definitively become a reality, but it can be grasped only in faith. The future things are now no longer the last things, but they are present, although they are hidden at the same time. Salvation has been offered to us, but we must patiently persevere and first bring forth more fruit. The elements which make up the eschatological life, namely joy, freedom, peace, love, truth, the glorification of God, are already present in the new heart into which the holy Pneuma was infused with faith (Rom. 5:5), so that Paul can once more proclaim with confidence and courage in the eighth chapter of his letter to the Romans (35–39):

> Who shall separate us from the love of Christ? Shall tribulation, or distress, or persecution, or hunger, or nakedness, or danger, or the sword? Even as it is written, "For thy sake we are put to death all the day long. We are regarded as sheep for the slaughter" (Ps. 43:23). But in all these things we overcome because of him who has loved us. For I am sure that neither death, nor life, nor angels, nor principalities, nor things present, nor things to come, nor powers, nor height, nor depth, nor any other creature will be able to separate us from the love of God, which is in Christ Jesus our Lord.

In fact, Paul not only had an idea of this, but experienced with his own body day after day that all the glory into which man is thrown when he believes is a hidden glory. The old aeon still lingers on, and the life of the community must take place under its laws. The hiddenness of the new is not only a concealment from the eyes and ears of the unbelieving world, but it is a concealment which goes right through the heart of the Christian. Faith does not take place in such a way that a man once and for all makes a confirming act of assent and then stubbornly maintains it. Faith requires a continually renewed, vital openness without which the personal encounter to which God calls man cannot take place.

Therefore the imperative "Be what you already are!" is a part of the epoch of salvation-history in which the eschatological is simultaneously present and hidden. For the time being the fullness can be obtained only if affliction is accepted along with it (cf. Mk. 10:29 f.). Sin, the law, and death are those forces which still threaten the freedom of the eschatological life. There still exist defection, disobedience, and temptation. It is still possible to betray the eschatological gifts of peace and freedom which have been entrusted to us. It is still necessary to bring to God our requests which the Lord's Prayer formulates; there are basically only two: that through God's activity the *basileia* might come, and that we might be suitable for it.

What makes up the eschatological freedom becomes understandable through the dialectic of the present and the future, the presence and the obscurity of the eschatological salvation: *to the extent that the Christian believes,* he is in Christ and abides in him, and God has taken up his abode in him. He has entered into a new existence, in which the non-saving trinity of the law, sin, and death is overcome. In this conquest is found what the New Testament calls freedom. "Where the Spirit of the Lord is, there is freedom" (2 Cor. 3:17). The Spirit of the Lord is the *Kyrios* himself who has become present in history. Ingo Hermann has presented this convincingly in his book about Pauline Christology.[3] Therefore where Christ is, there is freedom, namely, freedom from sin, the law and death.

But the characteristic and expression of the new life is not only this "freedom from," but also—and above all—the "freedom to." What purpose, then, does the eschatological freedom have? Paul gives us a surprising answer when he explains to the Galatians in his most enthusiastic testimony for the Christian's new freedom: "Therefore, brethren, we are not children of a slave-girl, but of the free woman—in virtue of the freedom wherewith Christ has made us free. Stand fast, and do not be caught under the yoke of slavery" (Gal. 4:31–5:1).

We obtain in faith, then, the freedom for freedom itself. He who has not previously become free in faith and been placed in freedom cannot exist for and in freedom. But after faith has opened the dimensions of freedom and has destroyed the old servitude to sin and death and to the law which bears witness to sin and death, then we are free for freedom; we can live according to the insight and discovery which Paul again describes in his eighth chapter to the Romans with the words: "Now we know that for those who love God all things work together unto good" (v. 28).

A "royal" freedom becomes visible here, freedom which is just as little of this world as the kingdom of which it is an expression and sign. In this eschatological freedom the distinctions of the old aeon are obsolete. Here social, racial and national differences no longer have a place. Here begins the Christian equality, for with God there is "no regard for the person" (Dt. 10:17; Wis. 6:8; Sir. 35:15; Matt. 22:16; Acts 10:34; Rom. 2:11; Jam. 2:1–9; 1 Pet. 1:17). A new fraternity and friendship are born out of the eschatological freedom, so that everyone who believes can with a free heart speak the words of Paul in the letter to the Galatians:

> But now that faith has come, we are no longer under a tutor. For you are all the children of God through faith in Christ Jesus. For all you who have been baptized into Christ, have put on Christ. There is neither "Jew nor Greek"; there is neither "slave nor free-man"; there is neither "male nor female." For you are all one in Christ Jesus. (Gal. 3:25–28.)

Here, then, is the Christian's primary responsibility for freedom: not to betray this totally unique and unsurpassed freedom of God. "Do not be caught under the yoke of slavery"—this warning of Paul (Gal. 5:1) describes the Christian obligation to preserve the freedom from sin, the law and death, to safeguard the freedom for freedom through all dangers and temptations. In fact, he is even to carry this freedom in the hope which defies all human hope, the hope of faith (Rom. 4:18), which awaits and longs for the manifestation of the dominion of God. We could also say: keep that one central commandment which alone still prevails in the new order, and you will be free. Then the same mystery would be stated with a different picture, for love is the real freedom. The refusal of eschatological-Christian love means falling back into the old aeon and into the middle of its law which brings sin and death. In the first letter of John we read:

> He who says that he is in the light, and hates his brother, is in the darkness still. He who loves his brother abides in the light, and for him there is no stumbling. But he who hates his brother is in the darkness, and walks in the darkness, and he does not know whither he goes; because the darkness has blinded his eyes. (1 John 2:9–11.)

That freedom is love and love freedom is the meaning of St. Augustine's famous words which are understandable only in the eschatological situation: *"Dilige, et quod vis fac"*—"Love, and then do what you will" (In the Letter of John to Parthos VII, 4, 8; PL 35, 2033).

There is no further need to stress that eschatological freedom does not mean moral anarchy, but that it keeps the quality of an obligation—and in such a way, in fact, that the obligatory quality is in the very freedom itself. For freedom which is not love and does not bring forth the fruit of the Spirit would not be freedom at all but only the old servitude again, which is now, of course, even worse. Eschatological freedom is itself the only law, so that St. James can speak of a "law of freedom" (Jam. 1:25; 2:12). By this he means the same as Paul, who contrasts the "law of the Pneuma" to the law of sin and death (Rom. 8:2). The Johannine Jesus declares the same experience of freedom, when concerning "truth" (which means the eschatological reality of the new life) he maintains that it will grant man freedom: "If you abide in my word, you shall be my disciples indeed, and you shall know the truth, and the truth shall make you free" (Jn. 8:31 f.).[4]

If we look back to what the New Testament says about eschatological freedom, we still have this to add: that new freedom, based on what it is, cannot be fundamentally violated by the powers of this world. It has its foundation in Christ himself and in faith in him; this foundation cannot be destroyed from the outside but only by man himself. Force and coercion might not be able to annihilate this freedom, but it is possible—and today no one fails to recognize this any more—for the eschatological freedom to be put under such intense pressures that the supreme commitment is demanded of man. We need only think of the first three centuries of the Church. They present a situation which is not simply to be eliminated from the history of this aeon, but necessarily belongs to it at least in principle. Today we know that there are temptations—I am not referring only to those outside the Church—which do not directly affect and touch upon eschatological freedom, but endeavor slowly and steadily to take away from it its foundation, namely faith.

With this we are already approaching the second form of freedom to be discussed. But first there is one more problem which deserves our attention and which may not be overlooked when Christian freedom is discussed. The eschatological freedom—as we have seen—is indeed present; however, it is not of this world and is therefore hidden and not in the realm of psychological experience. For that reason it must be stated and maintained that this freedom is in no way to be related to that problem which we can call "freedom in the Church."

For the eschatological kingdom of God, of which we have been speaking, does not quite coincide with the visible, hierarchical-juridical Church to which we belong. It is true that the Church as the community of the elect is and should be the place where the eschatological freedom can be met in the midst of this depraved and perverse generation (cf. Philip. 2:15). And even if, in the sense of Karl Rahner, one must speak of the Church as the tangible sacrament of the Pneuma (which is the freedom of our freedom),[5] nevertheless and for this very reason one may *not* approach the Church with the expectation that he will certainly find in her the fullness of that freedom.

For in this "meanwhile" the Church is subject to the laws of history and thus of the old aeon. Nevertheless, the manner in which the Church as the *Universitas fidelium* ("totality of the faithful") exerts herself in the cause of freedom—for the new freedom of course is not individualistic, but (as love) is directly related to the community—and the manner in which the Church bears witness to the eschatological freedom all throughout history could and must be perceptible to the world. It is quite obvious that here lies the responsibility of every individual and of the Church as a community, as the body of Christ, and here especially lies the responsibility of the hierarchy.

Insofar as the Church is inserted into the laws of the already antiquated and obsolete aeon, the eschatological freedom is also bound up in the form of the old. But it is not for this reason to be interpreted as lawless and capricious freedom, and certainly not as a license for evil (cf. 1 Petr. 2:16). It is also worth stressing that, precisely *because* the Church must bear and tolerate the contours of the old, freedom would be essentially better executed in her if she would achieve secular freedom within her walls. Granted this belongs to the old aeon, yet it belongs there in such a way that it preserves and presents the inalienable inheritance of God's creative act. Eschatological freedom can be active even in the midst of the secular unfreedom; this is also completely true of its fate even within the Church herself.

Yet the testimony to eschatological freedom which the Church is called to give in this world would be much more plausible if from the great richness of that freedom the entire fullness and depth of creaturely and secular freedom would find its place in the Church. This is especially true since the *full* revelation of the new spiritual freedom must remain reserved for the coming aeon. The more easily the eschatological freedom of the Christian forms itself and finds a place in the secular freedom of the Church, the more acceptable will be not only the testimony in faith of God's freedom, but also the testimony of faith itself.

Only when one sees in theological reflection, i.e., through an insight in and from faith, that all juridical-legal order and dogmatic teaching have their "meta-canonical" and "meta-dogmatic" domain within the Church can the law in the Church be properly understood.[6] Law in the Church no longer means the same thing as the law in the Old Covenant; much more than that, it indicates the New Covenant, the covenant written in the heart, the *analogia legis*: all law is to be considered only in the analogical sense. It has as its function the task of leading the Church as an earthly, visible community within the old aeon, and of preserving the eschatological freedom. A justification on the grounds of the law itself, i.e., merely for the fulfilment of the law, does not exist. Of sole importance is confidence in God, who entered into history and, bringing salvation, became present in the man Jesus. It is this attitude of confidence which the New Testament calls faith.

Freedom within the Church succumbs to the dialectic which is caused by the presence of the eschatological in world history. This means that misunderstandings and incorrect notions of freedom are always possible in the Church. Concerning this unfortunate situation, Karl Rahner writes:

> Since the Church is always also a Church made up of sinful men, even as far as the holders of her authority are concerned, she can also in her individual actions offend against her own principles and against the freedom of the individual both within and without. This has

happened often enough in the course of history. It can happen even today. And this is what the Church must guard against, for today more than ever she must be the champion of true freedom. But even by such individual offenses she does not become a totalitarian system. For she acts in these cases against her own proclaimed and practiced principles, whereas a really totalitarian system does not recognize such principles of freedom and dignity of the individual either expressly or tacitly, but on the contrary idolizes the collectivity and degrades the individual. But the Church must reckon with the real danger of giving scandal of an apparent totalitarianism.[7]

We know only too well today that the Church appears suspect to many of our contemporaries in the matter of freedom. It is unfortunate that Christians often find themselves in the position of having to assert that freedom and Christian (or more exactly Catholic) faith are completely compatible. People refer us to the 2414 canons of the Church's lawbook, to the Church's hesitant-to-opportunistic stand toward democracy (one thinks of the Maurras case),[8] and to her tendency to sympathize with authoritarian governments if they seem to feel sympathetic toward her and if they seem ready to compromise.[9] They refer to the Church's authority over the individual conscience (perhaps in connection with a political election), to the use of force in the medieval Church and in not a few missions in which they think it is possible to recognize the pure and distinguishing expression of the Catholic. They also refer us to the censure and supervision of scientific investigation, such as exegesis (but naturally not only exegesis), and to innumerable similar examples.

Here we cannot go into particulars to show that since the end of the Middle Ages the word "freedom" has become more and more the slogan of rationalistic and dechristianized modern thinking, and no longer sounds convincing in the mouth of the Church. The case of Galileo, which Bert Brecht took up, is symptomatic of the fate of freedom and of the free man within a Christianity which considers a particular historical form absolute. The attitude of the official Church toward the rising natural sciences finds a striking, no less unpleasant parallel in the relationship of the Church toward democratic and liberal ideas and aspirations, especially in the nineteenth and early twentieth centuries. It would be a disregard for the truth if we wished to ignore the undeniable fact concisely formulated by Karl Rahner: "St. Paul spoke of the freedom of the Christian. After that, this particular topic was no longer mentioned very much." [10]

The primary responsibility of the Christian for freedom demands that he live in the midst of the eschatological freedom according to the original source, namely the spirituality of the New Testament, and that he think and speak about it. It demands that in his free existence he give freedom a continually greater guarantee; it demands that freedom become almost second nature to him. In any case, says Rahner, freedom must be spoken of today, and he gives several reasons:

> For in times when there is no freedom, we search anxiously for it in whatever place we still hope to find it; and today people are listening more thoughtfully once again to the message of the Faith, especially such as it issued originally from the pages of the New Testament. We must speak of this subject nowadays, because one has become sensitive and delicate about transgressions against the holy spirit of freedom in the Church, since one does not at any cost wish to confuse the Church with a totalitarian collectivity.[11]

Now we shall turn to the consideration of secular freedom. This refers to what we feel and think when we speak of a "free world," of freedom in the political-social sphere and therefore in the terrestrial order. To approach the problem as such correctly, we must first put aside the theological aspect and proceed phenomenologically. This methodological observation is not merely an incidental pre-consideration. Rather the correct approach to the question is crucial for understanding the topic itself. The methodological abstinence from theology is not easy to observe, especially when one comes from the biblical-theological considerations we have sketched. Nevertheless it will prove useful just to accept and bear with this distinction of formal points of view here in the beginning.

World—an extremely ambiguous concept—is here understood as the totality of men insofar as they are present on the earth and constitute the open and communal quality of being-with-one-another (*Mitsein*). Man who makes up this world wants simply this one thing: he would like to live. He does not want to vegetate, but to live as a human primarily wants to live according to his nature and in a basically meaningful way. He wants to live, therefore, without fear and without want and sickness. Positively stated: man wants to live in a state of peace and happiness as imperturbably as possible, in a state of order—as a "necessary evil" which is not to be overlooked—and finally also in freedom (which is presumed and included in all the others).

These assertions are not exactly original; they sound like simple little idylls or simply like slogans. Nevertheless, just as soon as we ask only a few questions to examine the suppositions behind these statements, we find ourselves in almost insoluble difficulties, and the importance of the problem becomes only too clear.

Secular freedom, which we usually assume every man basically strives for and claims, obviously presupposes personal freedom. Secular freedom cannot be considered except as that state in which the individual man attains a maximum of his own being because and insofar as he possesses a unique, irreplaceable combination of specific characteristics which no one can take away, a unit in which the dignity of his person can be seen. And certainly this dignity of the person is exactly that which on the one hand today and always is questioned and even not recognized by threatening forces, and which on the other therefore must be convincingly proven to human thought to be legitimate so that it can receive some historical value.

Here we stand before an almost insurmountable difficulty. It concerns giving a foundation for the dignity of man. This is not to be done through some favorite solution, but rather on a basis which is as broad as possible, which is in principle open to all men, and which each man—disregarding the manifold differences which separate man—finds acceptable. This approach may not be understood as though human dignity could or should be once and for all guaranteed, explained, and where possible also recovered through a particular theory, philosophy, ideology or religion. Indeed one can never say that one must rationally define and understand the nature of freedom and human dignity before he is in a position to know what secular freedom is and how man achieves it.

With respect to the problem of time, Augustine in his *Confessions* wrote these famous lines (xi, 14):

> What is time? Who can easily and briefly explain this? Who can comprehend this even in thought, so as to express it in a word? Yet what do we discuss more familiarly and knowingly in conversation than time? Surely we understand it when we talk about it, and also understand it when we hear others talk about it. What, then, is time? If no one asks me, I know; if I want to explain it to someone who asks me, I do not know.[12]

What Augustine refers to here seems to be true for the problem of freedom also: thinking about freedom and speaking about it already presume a still unreflected, sketchy, but elementary knowledge of freedom. We call this "pre-understanding." The pre-understanding comprises very simple things; yet this simplicity plainly seems to be—and it is in this that its trans-historical actuality lies—what man continually strives after and longs for before all reflection only because of what he is and what he encounters.

The pre-understanding of freedom, the straightforward comprehension of what freedom means, in its most general form obviously refers to this: that every individual as such can perform or omit what he wants—the Greeks speak of *autopraxia,* the ability to work by one's self, to decide on one's own actions. It means that the individual can strive after happiness and peace, and work and drive himself for it as he considers right and necessary.[13] It means, finally, that this being-free, which presents itself to the pre-understanding already as a primary and pre-given *right,* in any case finds its limit where there are another or many other persons who are likewise free and have a claim to freedom in the same way that he does.

From these theoretical considerations it can be said: a community, whether it be a group, a nation, or the global "family of man," can realize secular freedom to the degree that each individual achieves his own freedom while preserving the other individuals' title to it. In fact, we can go a step further: the individual (not a complete unit, a personality isolated within himself, but a being made for society) achieves his true freedom only in the community, in the encounter with others.

Opposed to this true freedom, the alleged freedom of individualism appears to be silly isolation and servile dependence on the "I." Here need not be mentioned that at the very basis of the suggested principles differences of opinion, disputes, hardness and injustices might arise. To overcome such problems and to develop the principles of freedom in the most favorable proportion according to the situation is the function of politics. It is definite meanwhile, from the viewpoint of the philosophy of history, of political philosophy and of anthropology, that the principle of freedom as such is considered completely guaranteed.

What this central problem involves is where we find the biggest obstacle: that the pre-understanding of freedom, which we attributed to every man who experiences and understands himself as an individual (or, we can say, as a person), on one side is too general and vague for a world-wide society to be built on it; and on the other side what it wants to be and requires seems to be continually questionable.

Can we really trust the human pre-understanding of freedom? Can we rest assured that what man wants and strives after in a basic and primitive way, such as freedom, is "right" for him and the world; that it is true and good not only for the individual but for all? Does not an affirmative answer to these questions mean that we are of the opinion that men in themselves are always good, and that "nature," primitiveness, is all good and salvation for men? And finally there would be the question: Is it really so, that men are primitively directed toward freedom? Is not the goal basically sought by men much more "salvation" in some sort of transcendental or religious understanding of this concept, so that the personal and secular freedom takes second or third place in relation to this end?

For all those who have not come into contact with the personal-dialogue understanding of man which is common in biblical thought or for those who have rejected it and hold something else, does not the last and highest end consist in being absorbed into the totality of the clan, the nation, the collectivity, or else in becoming one with the All or with the Transcendence? When we consider the spirituality of India, China, Africa, and even Greek philosophy, the existential claims of the proposed questions become clearly acceptable.

Since it is here impossible to go into the numberless difficult problems individually, much less to find an objective, practical solution, I would like to indicate just a few ways in which one could approach the problem of secular freedom with at least a little meaning.

Above all, it evidently seems possible to admit that the pre-understanding of freedom cannot establish an order of secular freedom. In no way are there agreeing views on what one can perhaps call the "natural man." Neither Christianity, nor Buddhism, nor Marxism-Leninism (certainly not this one) is of the opinion that the individual is the way he discovers himself: always on the road of goodness and order, on a road which, so to speak, inevitably leads to freedom as long as he only stay on it. The optimism about nature of a Locke or Rousseau and the rationalism of the Enlightenment not only become shipwrecked in the realm of the absurd and of the demoniac in the world and in the heart of each individual; they also are incapable of conveying any generally essential information about the nature of man, since they presume to see clarities which do not exist; on the other hand they are not capable of preserving all of the dimensions of reality and of human experience, such as the holy and the beautiful.

When one considers the variety of philosophies and philosophers who are often struggling passionately with one another, and the variety of flagrantly divergent world outlooks, ideologies, and religions, then one may certainly say that de facto there is no *one* "truth" and with it no *one* foundation for freedom which would be recognizable for the whole world and thus binding on all. One certainly would observe that we are concerned here with the problem of the *binding force*. It naturally is far beyond me to dispute or bring into doubt the sense of philosophy and religion or their seriousness and necessity.

But it may also not be overlooked that philosophy itself, whether it be that of Socrates, Kant, or Wittgenstein, knows more or less explicitly how far it can go and where the area begins in which it can impart no more *definite* information, and where, therefore, it must remain silent. It cannot be overlooked that religions rest on freedom and assent, not on mathematically positive certainty which everyone can examine and follow.

Christianity itself, finally, stands or falls with the mystery of salvation-history, namely the mystery of election and vicarious redemption, and thus of faith also. Concerning this mystery, and in reference to philosophy since the days of Paul, Christianity explicitly explains that the wisdom of this world is "foolishness" (1 Cor. 1:20–25). In the language of St. Augustine and of the Middle Ages, philosophy, in spite of all its efforts and with all due respect to the ability of human reason, cannot attain the fundamentals of reality, the true *sapientia Dei,* since this can be received only from the hand of the God who reveals himself in history.

With the question of the foundation and the nature of secular freedom, we find ourselves facing a fundamental problem of human knowledge. Even when someone, such as the Christian, knows what the order of creation and the law of human creatures are and what they comprise, there still remains with respect to knowledge and its development the already stated problem: within the order of knowledge it is never possible, according to the testimony of philosophy, religion, and Christian faith also, to arrive at a general agreement among men concerning the ultimate principles, concerning being and its orders, and also, therefore, concerning a philosophical-metaphysical explanation of secular freedom.

Although a closer and more intensive agreement may be possible within wider cultures because of the history of these cultures (such as within the culture of Europe), in global dimensions agreement in the metaphysical-fundamental explanation of the meaning of human existence as well as of history and the world is neither to be found nor expected. Although this assertion is basically in no way surprising, it seemed advisable to present it here in this manner so as to draw the conclusions more clearly.

Since secular freedom cannot be postponed until men have agreed on what the principles of true human freedom are, there is only *one* answer, that is, to come to the best practical arrangement possible. Secular freedom can be achieved only through this, if at all: through an agreement on it and its essential requirements right in the midst of the great differences in principles.

But now we find ourselves in a vicious circle; for the necessity of an arrangement on secular freedom only raises anew the question of a comprehensive and binding knowledge, or at least a pre-understanding, of freedom, i.e., of man. If one wants to bring up the question of and search for a "minimal anthropology" here, then the chain of thoughts begins again at the same spot where we found ourselves earlier. But perhaps the posing of the question, or at least the situation in which the question is posed, has received a different nuance: it has left the phenomenological and philosophical basis, and now stands on the level of bare existence. Anyone who has lived without freedom experiences and knows directly what freedom on this level means, whether his experience has been that of his own body or in the mental confrontation with terror and fright which have caused our century to become a century of horror.

It becomes apparent that on the level of thinking (even with an appeal to the existential experience of freedom) we can in no way escape the vicious circle. Here the point has been reached where one—also philosophically seen—can no longer avoid a *decision*.

In the history of Western philosophy there is that strange operation of thought called the *regressus in infinitum,* the infinite regression. An example of this regression is found in the problem of causality, in which one proceeds from a definite given cause without reaching an end. If one does not *make* an end to this endless ascent (or better: regression) in the chain of causes by *deciding* courageously—as philosophy has done and considers legitimate—to force open the vicious circle and to accept a first, no-longer-caused cause, then an adequate knowledge is absolutely excluded.

In the face of the problem of freedom, one must, in my opinion, act in a similar way if he is to free himself from the vicious circle. It is valid, then, to accept the view that man's immediate recoil from terror and force is not a matter of his convenience, not an irrational and merely emotional reaction, and does not, therefore, reveal a bourgeois prejudice; rather this impulse reveals man and the essence of his given nature: namely, that he is a free person who possesses dignity, who must claim honor, and who has the right to be himself.

The person who makes this decision for the personal freedom and dignity of man understands at the same time the principles of secular freedom. Among modern thinkers there is no one who has thought out, perceived and spoken of the problem of freedom so frankly and radically as Albert Camus. In his great work *L'Homme révolté* (*The Rebel*), Camus establishes the fundamental dignity and right of man as a free being and formulates the basic law of secular freedom in the programmatic-sounding sentence: "The complicity and communication discovered by the revolt can live only in free dialogue." (Here is meant the revolt for the humane as distinguished from the destructive elements of all revolutions.)

Karl Jaspers, among many others, expressed himself in a similar way. In an essay called "Im Kampf mit dem Totalitarismus" ("In the Struggle with Totalitarianism"), he writes that the real struggle is "the fight for freedom within the free countries themselves. If what is fought for externally were lost within, then the battle would be senseless." [14]

Secular freedom becomes concrete for us in the political forms of democracy. Normally their philosophical assumptions are not clearly understood at all. In a frequently quoted speech about freedom, R. Guardini says: Democracy "is the most challenging and therefore the most dangerous of all political systems. This system continually grows from the free play of forces of persons with equal rights. The task of making it work is frightfully great, because there are not many who have an insight into its nature." [15]

What Camus understands by a world of "free dialogue," Jacques Maritain requires and supports in another way, proceeding from other presuppositions, but with the same intention as Camus and many others. He makes use of an old, often misused and misunderstood word: tolerance. For him tolerance does not mean only "patience" and "let be." He understands it in a much more positive sense, one could say, as an existential of being-with and "being-in-the-world." For Maritain tolerance means "human fellowship," a fellowship of freedom, of communication and of dialogue. It is only on this foundation apparently that secular freedom is possible.[16]

The numberless attempts to codify the common rights of man—

such as the one Janko Musulin brought together in the volume *Proklamationen der Freiheit* (Fischer Series: 1959)—are an impressive indication that a free world worthy of men can be found only on the basis of free dialogue.

But while nothing, as we have seen, can be proved scientifically and with conclusive assurance with respect to the nature and form of secular freedom and while it therefore involves a decision, the responsibility for secular freedom can still be discussed. In general it is good to renew our thinking of freedom continually and more basically, to speak of and discuss it, to venture into it in this way, and to love it more and more. One often has the impression that many recognize the value of freedom for the first time when it is threatened or lost. But now, what is the *Christian* responsibility for secular freedom in a world of free dialogue?

When we proceed from eschatological freedom, which characterizes the Christian as such, it appears that there is no visible connection to secular freedom. The Christian, insofar as he believes, is already in the eschatological reality; for this reason Paul can say: our *politeuma*, our citizenship, is in "heaven," in the kingdom of God (Phil. 3:20). In fact, the Christian cannot deny his "eschatological place" when he has to orient himself among and with non-Christians in his secular existence.

This means that the Christian, because of what he experiences through his faith, will always consider all human efforts for secular freedom with great skepticism and reserve. This he will do because he understands the temporality of earthly reality, which he always sees as something already antiquated and overcome. The Christian knows the mystery of history; he knows that man is destined for *one* end only. He also knows that this end is certainly not unworldly, a-cosmic or super-cosmic, but that it will be a new heaven and a new earth (Apoc. 21 and 22), in which God will be "all in all" (1 Cor. 15:28).

At the same time, however, the Christian knows that he would not have any insight into the mystery of history if it had not been given to him. He knows that he has been given everything that he has. Because the Christian knows of the gift-character of his incomparable freedom, he also knows what kind of inner tragedy all human attempts to found and bring about secular freedom must produce. And insofar as the Christian cannot remove himself from the structures of the old aeon (since God himself allows the old to linger on yet and therefore wills the dialectic which characterizes the time of the Church), he does not have the right to dispense himself from working along in the Sisyphos-like task of establishing order in the midst of secular institutions.

The essential motive for this obligation of the Christian forms the truth experienced in faith that this world is the creation of God, and as such has been made worthy in spite of all guilt of man, that it is renewed in Jesus Christ, and is to be accepted more ardently than before. The Christian also knows that the part of mankind which does not belong to the chosen old and new Israel is in no way removed from the God of history, but that it bears his law within itself (Rom. 1 and 2). He knows that when man obeys the dictates of his religions, philosophical systems and ethical efforts, he is straining for the one God.

Therefore, in spite of all the paradoxes, the Christian dares to trust that mankind can ardently move toward the secular freedom because it is destined for the future fullness of freedom. In the meantime there has entered into our field of vision what the utopians of the last century saw vaguely: a world government united and ordered in freedom. This strain of the human heart, which enthusiastically directs itself toward the one free world, need not at all be suspect and objectionable for the Christian. But rather the Christian—with all the reserve which he cannot give up—is able to recognize and help bring about the true meaning of the human ambition for secular freedom: that freedom points to the new world of eschatological freedom which God—taking and reforming this world—will erect.

Since the Christian is able to recognize all this through his faith, he is responsible before God for the fate of secular freedom in this historical hour. His faith obliges him to strive for the world of free dialogue in which each human is capable of existing as a free person with honor and dignity. The solidarity with humanity, into which the Christian sees himself inserted, must occasionally even cause him to restrain himself, so that he does not betray eschatological freedom as well as secular freedom by a know-it-all attitude in daily politics, by a wrong idea of the relation of Church and State (caused in turn by a medieval misunderstanding of the kingdom of God), or even by military and crypto-psychological use of power. Without solidarity in the struggle for secular freedom, the Church would not only remain an unreliable partner with respect to this freedom, but, much worse, she could not give testimony to the eschatological freedom, which is the testimony of faith itself.

Here it becomes evident that the Christian's responsibility for both eschatological and secular freedom is intrinsically connected: the responsibility for secular freedom is the sign of the existence practiced and rooted in eschatological freedom. At the same time it is true that the eschatological freedom, while it makes the Christian free for the solidarity with all in the establishment of secular freedom, also preserves him from mythologizing this freedom and from a presumptuous expectation of it.

Secular freedom is exposed to many dangers today. The acutest occurs when human hope, with absolute exclusiveness and in the midst of constant disregard for death and other elementary experiences of existence, concerns itself only with the present form of the earth and comes up with the claim to have recognized with scientific exactness the nature of freedom and of being human. On account of this it also comes up with the demand to be legitimated by history and thus by humanity itself, and the demand if need be to force humanity to its happiness and to its freedom. In the face of such a radically attacking threat, a purely spiritual justification of true secular freedom is not sufficient; rather, mankind is in the fatal situation of having to use means it detests most deeply. It is important to see that this limitation forces itself upon the scene because and for the sake of the nature of secular freedom.

In this situation it will also be more clearly seen to what degree eschatological freedom remains hidden, how intensively the Christian, contrary to his better self, remains subject to the laws of the old aeon. Eschatological freedom as such cannot be defended on the level of secular freedom, but for the sake of man and creation, secular freedom needs protection from "unfreedom." The tension and conflicts in conscience which can arise here are hard, unsentimental, and hardly bearable.

According to all this, the Christian's responsibility for freedom is so strongly challenged and put under such pressure that it almost seems impossible for Christianity—today more than ever—to be able to meet it. Nevertheless, there are some grounds for confidence. When we say and believe that man is created by God for freedom and in Christ has become free for freedom, it is not a mere theoretical disclosure; rather it denotes a reality which is hidden in history but which is nevertheless effective.

More exactly seen, the basis of Christian hope lies in the salvation-history mystery of vicarious redemption. Joseph Ratzinger has emphatically shown [17] that vicarious redemption is the key to understanding history, the Church, election, and salvation: what the few carry out by virtue of faith bears fruit for history, for he who believes is one with Christ and is empowered to cooperate with him in the great work of the history of salvation. He who as a Christian stands up for freedom individually also stands up for the freedom of all. He who as a Christian takes upon himself and bears responsibility for eschatological and secular freedom helps history and the world reach Omega Point, which means that fulfilment in which freedom is endless.

NOTES

[1] The following exposition is an address delivered in Berlin in October, 1961.

[2] I am aware that the following exposition remains incomplete in many respects, and that it can (and is intended to) be merely a stimulus which raises some frequently forgotten aspects and brings them into discussion.

[3] *Kyrios und Pneuma, Studien zur Christologie der Paulinsichen Hauptbriefe* (Munich: 1961). Cf. p. 113: "The Pneuma is the medium of the encounter between God and man."

[4] There is a need to indicate that this statement of John presents neither a political nor a philosophical insight.

[5] "Freedom in the Church," in: *Theological Investigations II* (Baltimore: Helicon, 1963), p. 96.

[6] Cf. G. Söhngen, "Der metakanonistische Bereich, ein rechtstheologischer Begriff," in: *Die Kirche und ihre Ämter und Stände* (Cologne: 1960), pp. 276–85.

[7] *Op. cit.*, pp. 99–100.

[8] Cf. E. Nolte, "Die Action Française," in: *Vierteljahrshefte für Zeitgeschichte* 9 (1961), pp. 124–65.

[9] Cf. E. W. Bockenforde, "Der deutsche Katholizismus im Jahre 1933," in: *Hochland* 53 (1960/61), pp. 215–39, and the heated reaction this article gave rise to.

[10] *Op. cit.*, p. 89. Certainly there was a great deal of loud discussion about freedom at the time of the Reformation, but that cannot be handled here.

[11] *Ibid.*, p. 90.

[12] *The Confessions of St. Augustine* (Garden City: 1962), p. 287.

[13] Cf. R. L. Bruckberger, *Image of America* (New York: 1959), a work well worth reading, especially the interpretation of the philosophi-

cal background and the revolutionary character of (the American) democracy.

[14] In *Philosophie und Welt* (Munich: 1958), p. 96.

[15] "Freiheit, Eine Gedenkrede" (lecture in Munich, July 19, 1960), in: *Sorge um den Menschen* (Würzburg: 1962), pp. 133 ff.

[16] Cf. J. Maritain, "Truth and Human Fellowship" (lecture at Princeton University), in: *On the Use of Philosophy* (Princeton University Press: 1957).

[17] "Die neuen Heiden und die Kirche," in: *Hochland* 51 (1958/59), pp. 9–11. Cf. also Ratzinger's article "Stellvertretung," in: *Handbuch theologischer Grundbegriffe II*, ed. H. Fries (Munich: 1963), pp. 566–75.

Christianity and the "New Man"

The Christian Faith and Utopian Views About the Future of This World

by KARL RAHNER, S.J.

CHRISTIANITY IS A RELIGION with an eschatology; it looks into the future; it makes binding pronouncements about what is to come both by explaining what will come and by looking on these future events as the decisive guiding principles of action in the present. Indeed, Christianity declares that with the incarnation of the eternal Word of God in Jesus Christ, the last age has already begun, that the future has already been decided as to its final sense and content, and that now it only requires that which is already and remains to be revealed.

Christianity no longer knows any ultimately open salvation-history but declares that—since the coming of Jesus Christ who is today, yesterday and in all eternity—the end of the ages is really already present and that we live, therefore, in the last ages, in the fullness of time. One thing only remains for us and that is to await the coming of the Lord in glory, even though—reckoned in earthly measurements of time—this period of waiting may appear long to us and even though thousands upon thousands of years on this earth may pass through this one moment of the silence of the end of time before the real and ultimate end finally dawns. Christianity understands itself as the religion of the future, as the religion of the new and eternal man.

Christianity cannot be indifferent, therefore, in the face of an interpretation, planning and utopian ideal of the future which originates outside her and which tries to determine man's present attitude in view of his future. It cannot be doubted, however, that the spiritual situation of man today is essentially determined by the blueprint of the new man of the future. The man of today feels himself to a larger extent to be someone who must overcome himself in order to prepare himself for a new and quite different future. He feels himself to be someone whose present can be justified only as the condition of his future, though this future which justifies him is not conceived—eschatologically—as the gift of God dissolving temporal history but as something which man himself creates and conquers for himself. Hence, the question as to how these two conceptions of the future are related to one another is an unavoidable and, for the Christian, an absolutely decisive one.

Before tackling this question directly, we must make at least some attempt to give a clearer picture of modern, extra-Christian thought concerning the future, so that we may know with what we are really comparing the Christian eschatology. Naturally, the "picture of the new man" can be sketched here only in its most formal traits. Yet this picture of the new man cannot be simply presupposed as known, at least not from *those* points of view which must be our special concern here. We presuppose in this that this "new man" is already present today in his beginnings, in the sense that, to some extent at least, his further developments and final form can already be divined. Furthermore, in describing the new man, we are not concerned with laying down a binding, systematic view of the characteristics exposed.

The man of today, and even more so the man of tomorrow, is the man of a history unified the world over, the man of a global space for life and hence the man of a world in which everyone is dependent on absolutely everyone else. The "United Nations" organization is a small indication of this. And the boundary lines drawn by the various "curtains" today do not limit the meaning of what has just been said, for one's enemies are usually "closer" to oneself—in the sense of being more decisive for one's own destiny —than one's friends.

Whereas in the past (prescinding from the only hypothetically and approximately ascertainable beginning of the human race) the history of individual peoples, and hence of individuals, was more or less clearly divided up by historical vacua; thus, for instance, what was happening at the time in the empire of the Incas was quite immaterial to the history of fourteenth-century Europe; today all the histories of different peoples are part and parcel of the one, real world-history. The "field" which determines the fate of the individual today is, not merely physically but also historically, the whole earth. The present and the history of individuals have become the present and the history of all, and vice versa.

The man of today and tomorrow is the man of technology, of automation and cybernetics. This means, in our present context, that man is no longer (or at least no longer to any large extent) the man who simply lives out his existence according to the given pattern of nature in an equally pre-existent environment, but someone who fashions his own environment. Man now inserts an external world made by himself in between himself (eking out and asserting his existence both physically and spiritually) and "nature" (i.e., the physically and biologically tangible environment which is the condition for man's own existence).

It is of course true that there has never been a man without any culture, a man—in other words—who was able to live like an animal in the sense that his struggle for existence (by procreation and upbringing of offspring, protection against the dangers of his environment, etc.) was related immediately to a purely pre-established reality, as in the case of the animal. But in the past, culture, understood as something external, has on the whole consisted merely in such slight modifications of man's natural environment as this environment itself permitted: it consisted merely in the *utilization* of animals and plants in a certain systematic way, without any deliberate transformation of nature in the inorganic and organic world in the light of freely chosen ends and under rational control.

Life today, which has been thus transformed, always and everywhere manifests the reason why such a transformed life in an environment determined by ourselves is possible: the modern rationality of Western man, his calculated planning, the disappearance of the feeling of awe which used to be inherent in the experience of the world itself, and the "profanation" of the world, turning it into the raw material of human activity, an idea which—starting with the Western world—has become the determining presupposition of any consideration of the raison d'être of the whole world and of humanity.

The man of today is not, however, merely the man of the rational, calculating creation of his own space of existence—the *homo faber*. Unlike the man of previous ages (especially since the start of the modern fashion of "turning in on the subject"), the man of today is not merely the man given to that sort of rational reflection on himself in which (at least at the first and important appearance) the object of reflection is not altered by the fact of reflection.

Rather, he is someone who applies his technical, planning power of transformation even to himself—someone who makes himself the object of his own manipulations. He no longer simply takes stock of himself, but changes himself; he contents himself neither with steering by his own history merely the alteration of his sphere of existence nor with the mere actualization of those possibilities which have always offered themselves to man in his commerce with his fellow men both in peace and in war. The subject is becoming its own most proper object; man is becoming his own creator.

It does not matter in the meantime that for many different reasons and in many different respects these possibilities of a planned self-alteration and adaptation are as yet relatively few. The important thing is that man has thought of the idea of such a transformation, that he already sees possibilities of realizing this idea and indeed has already begun to realize it. Against this background must be seen the Freudian depth-psychology, birth-control, human eugenics, the transformations of man, based on Pavlov's psychology, which override the free judgments and decisions of man in the Communistic world and which are practiced—in somewhat more careful doses—even in the West (one need only think here of the techniques of propaganda, advertising, etc.).

This man of the unified, planetary living-space which is to be extended even beyond the earth—the man who does not simply accept the world around him but creates it and who regards himself as merely the starting point and raw material for what he wants to make of himself in accordance with his own plans—has for these very reasons the impression of standing at a beginning, of being the beginning of the new man, conceived as a kind of superman who will show clearly for the first time what man really is. What comments are to be made on this ideology of the new man, if the situation and program just described are looked at from the point of view of the Christian faith?

I

Christianity has no predictions to make, no program and no clear-cut prescriptions for the future of man in this world; it knows from the very start that man does not have them either and that he (and hence also Christianity itself) must therefore go unprotected into the dark venture of his intramundane future. The eschatology of Christianity is no intramundane utopia; it sets no intramundane tasks and goals. As a consequence, the Christian is not given any concrete directions for his life in this world as such, which could relieve him of the anguish of planning the future and of the burden of his passage into the dark unknown. He has the moral law of nature and of the gospel. But he himself must convert these general principles into concrete imperatives which themselves are not merely applications of these principles to a static material of moral action with which he has to deal, but also represent decisions about some definite plan of action and about the choice of different possibilities—none of which can be clearly deduced from these general principles.

By the fact that man changes himself and his environment—and by the fact that, since paradoxically but truly this planning does not make all this any the less unpredictable but rather increases the uncertainty in equal proportion to the extent of the planning, these alterations themselves have in their turn the character of something unpredictable, of trial and a wandering into the uncertain—ever new and surprising tasks are imposed by very reason of the principles advocated by Christianity, tasks which earlier Christianity could not have dreamed of and which require a long, laborious process of acclimatization for the Christian and the Church before they can be mastered at all.

Yet it is not as if this passage into the unpredictable future were unimportant for Christianity itself and of no significance for Christianity both as a Church and as the Christian life of individuals and nations. Truly realized Christianity is always the achieved synthesis on each occasion of the message of the gospel and of the grace of Christ, on the one hand, and of the concrete situation in which the gospel is to be lived, on the other. This situation is always new and surprising. Consequently the intramundane and Christian task of the Christian is really and truly a *problem* whose solution must be looked for laboriously amid surprises, pains, fruitless and false steps, false detachment and restoring, timidly conservative reserve and false fascinations with novelties.

Thus the Christian too may stand frightened and fascinated before the future of intramundane tasks opening out before him. He too may feel himself called to action and to criticism, in brotherly union with all those others who salute this future and who know themselves called to bring it about. Since the mastering of the intramundane situation represents a task (insofar as this is possible for man) which is also really Christian—because eternal life must be effected in time—it is, sadly perhaps, possible to show that the Christians of this day and age occupy themselves far too little with the programming of man's future in this world, as if this did not present any problems or could safely be left to the non-Christians.

It is indeed true and a fact of decisive importance that the gospel does not offer or intend to offer any ready-made plan for the future and that the Church cannot give us any clear-cut and binding ideas about such programming. But this in no way means that *every* programming for the future—whatever it may be—can be reconciled with the Christian spirit and life and with the nature of man of which Christianity is the custodian.

Hence, it does not mean that even in their practical life Christians have no duty or obligation with regard to such practical programming. It is absolutely possible for Christians to have a task as Christian individuals which the Church as such does not have. And it may seem that Christians do not have a clear, courageous and infectious enough conception and love of this planning of the future and of these demands—which go beyond the abstract principles of the unchanging gospel—and that they merely seek to defend the spirit of the gospel by a *defensive criticism* of the dangers of plans for the future and of intramundane ideologies.

Nevertheless, it remains true to say that the Christian as such is not given any clear prescriptions by the gospel as to how the future is to look or will in fact look. He is a pilgrim on this earth, advancing into the uncertain and going out to venture in brotherly union with all those who plan the future of this world, and he may quite legitimately feel proud of being that creature who plans himself and of being the place (called "spirit" and "freedom") where the great world-machine not only runs its course in exalted clarity but also begins to steer itself.

II

Christianity draws man's attention to the fact that, while he is under the impression of standing on the threshold of a new and unheard-of future, this future too will constantly lead him back to himself as the finite creature he is. This future, planned by himself and to be built by himself, is inevitably finite for the Christian; he already recognizes, experiences and suffers it as something finite in advance. In other words, the future too is built out of materials with definite structures whose finite nature also sets internal limits to the possibilities of the future and renders them finite. Man does indeed over and over again express surprise at how he has underestimated his own possibilities, at how the world is greater than he had thought, at how new avenues open out to possibilities which he had up until now regarded as utopian.

Certainly it is dangerous in many respects to declare something to be impossible; for many times in the past such declarations have been the beginnings of successful efforts to make the impossible come true. Nevertheless, man is not and will never be the creator who creates omnipotently out of nothing—he is and will always be the creature who creates out of himself and out of the already existing realities of the world around him. And he and the reality surrounding him have structures and laws; these already existing realities, together with their determined structures, form the a priori law of what they can become.

These essential structures are not—this modern man has learned and this also differentiates him from the man of earlier ages, including the Christian Middle Ages—a static barrier which prevents any genuine process of becoming and change and being-changed.

These essential structures are most certainly endowed with an inner dynamism toward development. But precisely in this way they also form the law according to which this development takes place and the horizon within which the history of this development runs its course. And no matter how much this course may take us into the boundless, there are twists and turns in it which betray the finite and created nature of this course of becoming, the becoming to which it remains necessarily subject.

There are many such a priori, inevitable elements in the finite nature of man. There is his spatio-temporality: even if man should conquer a new part of the world for himself outside his earth (and if we stop to think, are we not still very far from this being true?), he will always face the immensity of the universe as someone who begins his short span of existence from the earth and not from anywhere else.

Then there is man's biological constitution together with all the limitations this entails: the different stages of life, his dependence on nourishment, the finite nature of his brain—the storehouse of his activities—which provide the basis for what he can really experience and by which alone in the final analysis all other (artificial) stores of usable content become really interesting for him, in the same way that someone finds interest only in *those* books of a library which he reads (and not in those which he can read) or at most in those which he could read *without* having to give up the reading of others. And finally there is the limited nature of his life which ends in death.

This brings us then to the most irrevocable and clearest limit of man: he dies, he has a beginning and an end, and this means that absolutely everything which lies within these "brackets" is under the relentless sign of the finite. We are able to prolong human life and in fact have already done so. But what a laughable alteration would it really be if we were all to become 120 or 180 years old? Who has ever claimed or prophesied that he could do more?

And who—even if he were to give but a little thought to such a utopian idea—could even merely hope or wish to live forever in the kind of human existence which is the only one given to us? The *inner* finiteness of human existence would turn the *external* endlessness of life into utter madness—into the existence of the eternally wandering Jew—and into damnation, since what is unique in a finite sense is impressive and sweet only if, and because, it is not always available; a time which I could really have to infinity whenever I liked, condemns the content of each moment to absolute indifference, since it is absolutely repeatable. And then: what significance does it have for *me*—I who will die—if I could help to make it possible that at some future date a man may be bred who will never die any more? None whatsoever! But we will have to come back to this point later on.

No, the message of Christianity about the finite and created nature of man remains true even today. And the more it might be possible to achieve what today lies still in a utopian future, the less could this achievement blind us to the finiteness of the achieved or deaden the pain of this finiteness. This is all the more true since it is an unproved supposition that the possibility and the pace of new developments experienced by us today could never be followed by a certain phase of stagnation, or that the time of pre-planned and self-directed development—once started—must unceasingly flow on in ever greater acceleration to ever new shores.

It is just as possible that the development may, as it were, stagnate again (although this time on the higher level reached by then) just as it did in many earlier centuries as far as the progress of technology and the external style of living were concerned. And since society is always and inevitably composed of individuals (it being quite indifferent for this whether one adopts an individualist or Communist view of the exact relationship between the individual and society), the finiteness we have spoken of determines not only the existence of the individual as such but permeates right through the life of society.

Since society cannot pass on culture by biological heredity, it must to a great extent always begin again at the beginning. No matter how cunningly exact and comprehensive our planning may possibly be, it will never be adequate but will always produce surprises and failures, for a finite consciousness inevitably contains more objectively unreflected elements than elements which have been fully reflected upon. This is so even simply because the act of reflection cannot itself be reflected and yet a great deal about its content depends on it and on its characteristics.

Indeed, it may be that there is an absolutely finite optimum of what can be planned. All planning must work with unplanned factors; the proportion between the unplanned factors, which are of practical importance for the result of the plan, and the planned factors and their certainty for the planned result is variable; it can easily happen that the more complicated plan which is calculated to avoid more mistakes works out worse in practice than the simple plan which works with less explicit factors. To put it more simply still: even the culture and civilization of society, which is seemingly growing into infinity, will always remain conditioned by the individual—in other words, by the finiteness of his consciousness, by the limited number of individuals and the finite nature of the life of individuals. And so this culture and civilization remain finite.

It can happen, of course, that this finiteness does not appear—at least not explicitly—in all its existential radicality in the consciousness of the individual and in the commonly expressed opinion of a group or of an age, etc. Perhaps the movement is experienced enthusiastically as a movement into infinity even on account of its very presence alone, for the simple reason that one has overlooked the fact that a movement—even though its limitation is not clearly experienced—never attains anything beyond what is finite, and because one has not adverted to the fact that an infinite potency does not by any means promise an infinite act.

In any case, this intoxicating experience of infinity will always end up in cruel disillusionment—at the latest in death. And the pretension to infinity found in man—which according to the teaching of Christianity stems from the infinite promise of grace—will always weigh up again what has been, and what can be, achieved in this world and will always find it to be of too little weight.

III

Christianity knows an individual and existential notion of time which those who dream of a future paradise on this earth do not possess, and the lack of any such notion shows the latter conception to be insufficient. Let us take a closer look at this. It is said—and no doubt rightly—that the future has already begun. It is said, both in the West and in the East, that we are moving toward a glorious age: man will conquer outer space, there will be enough food for everyone, there will no longer be any underdeveloped and undernourished countries, everybody will have what is required to fulfil his needs, class distinction will be abolished.

The Christian must not indeed act as if all these plans for the future are proved wrong simply by his declaring skeptically that paradise is not to be found in this world. Anyone who simply counters such ardent dreams of the future with sober skepticism is—presumably—not experiencing hunger, is not at present in danger of cancer and hence is not particularly interested in finding the means by which medicine may at last conquer this disease. Yet the Christian is right in the long run when he points out that this happy future has not yet arrived, that he himself will not be alive to experience it and that he cannot agree that the question of *his* existence is solved by saying that it will be solved for others in the future.

The fight for a better future does consciously or unconsciously live on an evaluation of man, and even of the individual, which attributes an absolute value to man as a spiritual person. And this is quite right. For why should someone living today sacrifice himself for someone in the future if the future individual is just as insignificant as the present-day individual is thought to be, and if the present-day individual could be sacrificed precisely because he is insignificant?

The Communist who today sacrifices himself in true freedom and quite unselfishly for those who will come after him, affirms by this very fact that he as a person and those future persons have an absolute value, whether he admits this explicitly to himself or not. Anyone who affirms someone else to be of absolute value does the same for himself. He does not consider himself to be necessary in his biological existence, but he does acknowledge himself to be necessary in the dimension in which he takes the decision of self-sacrificing affirmation, namely, as a free, personal spirit.

Any conception which regards the future as something which does not simply come about by itself but must be conquered by sacrifice, acknowledges implicitly what Christianity affirms explicitly: the future of the human, spiritual person in no way only lies in *that* future which will be present at some later date but is the eternity which is brought about as the result of the spiritual act of the person.

Christianity is quite right in saying that there is a personal, existential time which is the coming-to-be of the unconditioned finality of the free decision and of existence—and which works in time by overcoming merely continuous time. All ideologies concerned with the future which declare that the future that is yet to come in a *temporal way* is something absolutely inevitable and not something to be merely overcome in the same way as the bare present must be overcome, borrow this notion of the absolute nature of the future from that future which is really absolute, namely, the future of the free person.

This future of the free person will not come later on but is present in the spiritual person and his free act; it realizes itself in the sphere where life—open to the bounded in its linear temporal nature—is brought to an end by biological processes. If every existing thing were completely subject to that time, whose every moment is indifferent since it passes away into an equally indifferent later moment in time which in turn unmasks its own insignificance by disappearing once more in the next moment, then we would have no reason for preferring a future to the present which is no longer the future of the one who has this preference. The present is necessarily the only true and valid reality for someone who is simply passing away, if indeed he ever becomes at all conscious of himself and of his transitoriness. Only if there is a future of the personal individual spirit is there any real sense in fighting for a better future in this world for those who will come after us.

It is clear from these few cursory remarks that Christianity has a notion of time in its teaching about the individual and freely achieved finality of the person, which goes beyond the notion of time employed by any ideology and utopian view which—concerned only with this world and its future—thinks of time purely as a sort of line passing into what is yet to come. The Christian notion of time goes much further, for it provides whatever is genuine and morally justified in these ideologies about the future with the only foundation which will really hold water, and opens up a supramundane and suprahistorical "future" for man which is above the eternal flux of time, namely, eternal life which finds its temporal expression and proof in time and which is the only future that has really already begun even now, in every present moment of the free decision of believing love.

IV

Christianity has already surpassed all ideologies about the future and all utopias in a completely different way still—by its teaching on the incarnation of the eternal Word of God and the universal salvation already ushered in by this event. It is first of all very striking how pale and shallow everything becomes when those who believe in an intramundane future (conceived as a beatifying paradise and as the triumph of successful man thus bringing nature to its own proper completion) are asked to explain what this future they are striving for will really look like.

We will be able to circumnavigate the moon and will perhaps be able to land on Mars; Russia will have surpassed America's meat production; no one will suffer want any more; there will be enough time and money to give everyone the best education possible and to offer him all the cultural goods he desires, etc.; everyone will have everything he needs. And so the catalogue goes. But one gets the impression that all this is not very much different from what is already possible and in part already normal even today—in other words, that the "new man" will look hopelessly like the old one.

In contrast to this (not in the sense of mere contradiction but of a message regarding a completely new and different dimension of human existence), Christianity proclaims that man can have a direct encounter with the Infinite and the Absolute—with the One who from the outset surpasses everything finite and who is not constituted piecemeal by finite moments of progression. Christianity proclaims that man's business is with God himself; it tells us that this unspeakable mystery we call God does not merely remain the ever-distant horizon of our experiences of the transcendent as well as of the finite, but that the Infinity as such can also descend into the heart of man which is "finite" in such a way that it can nevertheless be given the grace of this unspeakable Infinity.

Christianity proclaims that we will come face to face with the Infinity of absolute Reality, with the inaccessible Light and the Incomprehensible who is infinitely beatifying life. It proclaims that this personal Infinity has already begun to assume the finiteness of the spiritual, personal world of man into his eternal life by the fact that Jesus Christ, the eternal Word of God, has already made this finite quest for the infinity of God (i.e., human nature) his own and has replied to it with the answer of the eternal Word.

Christianity teaches that God has already broken up the world and has already opened up an exit for it which leads into his own Infinity, even while the world still pursues its course along the interiorly crooked paths of its finite history—even while it is still subject to change by the fact that it can only replace *one* finite thing with another finite thing which, even though it may be better than what has gone before, will always remain both a promise and a disappointment and nothing more for that spirit who recognizes and suffers his finiteness. In the actual world, creation no longer means merely the bringing-into-existence of something out of an infinite foundation and the perpetual keeping of this originated reality distant from its incommunicable source, but means rather the production of the finite as something on which the Infinite lavishes himself in the form of Love.

This history of the infinite endowment of the creature with God's reality is indeed primarily the history of the personal spirit and certainly takes place primarily as the existential history of faith across the temporal progress of the history of the material cosmos. Yet this fulfilment of the finite by the infinity of God does nevertheless refer to the whole of created reality. Christianity knows no history of the spirit and of existence which could be conceived simply as overcoming and repulsing the material, and for which the history of the cosmos would at most offer the external stage on which the drama of the personal spirit and his divine endowment would enact itself in such a way that, when the play is over, the players would leave the stage and would leave it dead and empty and abandoned to itself.

After all, the history in which God himself takes part by entering personally into it is the history of God's becoming *flesh* and not only the coming of a merely ideological spirit. Christianity professes belief in the resurrection of the body and means by this that in the last analysis there is only *one* history and *one* end of *everything*, and that everything reaches its end only once it has taken possession of God himself. Christianity, indeed, only conceives and knows a matter which is different from spirit and out of which the spirit cannot simply develop as the very product proper to that matter, as is taught by dialectical materialism. Yet Christianity knows only a matter which is created and exists from the very start *by* the Spirit who is called God and *for* the spirit called man, in order to make spiritual, personal life possible and to act as a basis for such a life.

The spirit is not a stranger in a spirit-less world which follows its own paths quite unconcerned about this spirit, but rather this material world is the corporeal presence of the spirit, the extended being of man, and has therefore ultimately the same end and destiny as man. Even in eternity—when the spirit will be fully achieved—the material world will be the expression of this achieved spirit and hence will participate in the final state of this spirit in—as we say—a "glorified" manner. Hence we profess that the end will be a new earth and a new heaven.

We cannot say very much about this achieved, final state of the bodily, mundane spirit: and this precisely because every intramundane achievement could only be an achievement constituted of finite elements, and so not at all an absolute achievement. Precisely because God's message has given us the boldness to believe in an infinite achievement, the only way we can in principle describe this consummation in its material content is to say that God himself will be this consummation. And since God, the Infinite, is the mystery which can be named and called upon only by a *via negationis* and by pointing silently beyond anything which can be put into words, we can speak of this consummation only negatively in images and likenesses and in speechless reference to absolute Transcendence.

Our consummation, therefore, is not fitted to become the subject of party tirades, of glowing imagery, of plastic descriptions or utopian conceptions. And when the man of today reads the old descriptions of this consummation which were less burdened with the images of an apparently intramundane utopia but employed an apocalyptic rather than a properly eschatological imagery, he will feel less at ease in all this than the man of previous ages. He will "demythologize" in a manner both justifiable and necessary if he is to be truly orthodox. This does not mean, however, that he has thereby in any real sense moved further away from an understanding of the reality itself. On the contrary, he knows that the truly infinite nature of his consummation is something unspeakable embracing all the dimensions of his being (but each of them in its own way) and that it—precisely as achievement by God and in God himself—is something unattainable by man himself, something given to him as a gratuitous gift of pure grace.

By the fact that this coming of God himself is the true and the only infinite future of man, Christianity has always already infinitely surpassed all intramundane ideologies and utopias about the future. The infinity of this future which is already beginning embraces all intramundane futures; it does not exclude them, nor does it make them unlawful (as long as they are mindful of their limitations as created forms). Again, it is not as if the man who believes in the coming of God's future can no longer acknowledge himself to be called to cooperate in working for these intramundane futures; and his supramundane, eschatological outlook does not necessarily have to dampen his inner urge for such cooperation.

Even if we leave it an open question whether God does not in fact realize certain things (which he wishes to be achieved in the world) through the *guilt* of men and not through the actions of those who love him, it must still be said in principle that the Christian is absolutely justified and qualified—and indeed to a certain extent obliged—to take an active part in working for the progress of the human race and thus of the world, by developing his own immanent powers and those of the world. For the consummation to be brought about by God does not, in the last analysis, expect a dead but a living humanity which has gone to its very limits and so is burst open by salvation from above by developing its own powers. For man's finiteness and the essential tragedy and fruitlessness of all human history, inherent in all finite development, become manifest more relentlessly in this way than it would in a purely static world.

V

However much the Christian—the man of a divine future—is a citizen of the world to come and not merely the child and supporter of the present world, and however great the development of this world into the unlimited may be thought to be, the Christian must nevertheless live at present in this world which is always a world of a future already begun: a new world full of earthly goals, tasks and dangers. It would be a complete misunderstanding of everything that has been said so far, if one were to think that a Christian may withdraw into some dead corner of world-history, as it were, or that he is someone belonging historically or socially to that class of people to be found in every history and development, i.e., the people of yesterday who are no longer really attuned to the times—the adherents to what is over and done with—the conservatives who weep for the good old days.

It cannot be denied, of course, that the good Christian of Christianity often gives this impression. It is true that Christianity has not been given any guarantee by God that it will be unable to sleep through the present. Christianity can be old-fashioned, it can forget that the old truths and the values of yesterday can be defended only if and when one conquers a new future. And it has actually to a great extent fallen into this error, so that today's Christianity often gives rise to the painful impression that it is running mopishly and in a disgusted, critical mood behind the carriage in which the human race drives into a new future.

One gets the impression that God's immense revolution in his history, in which he lets the world burn up in his own infinite fire, rests on the shoulders of people who really put their trust in what has proved itself in the past, although this is ultimately also only of this world and hence brittle, ambiguous and transitory, just as what is still to come in this world. Why are Christians so often to be found only on the conservative side? They really would not be forced to subscribe to other people's plans for the future if these are unchristian and inhuman. But then they ought also to have their own list of imperatives for the next couple of centuries and not just for eternity—and not merely general principles which they declare to be valid yesterday, tomorrow and always.

All these facts do not need to be covered up but can be admitted without any qualms. They do not alter the *principle*, however, that the Christian can truly achieve his own proper Christian being completely and fully only if he lives evidently and unconditionally in the present and in the future, and not merely in the past. This does not mean that someone who is going to build a new future in this world has already lived and proved his Christianity by this fact alone. But it is part of the convictions of a full Christian life that Christian faith and morality are in fact and of necessity exercised by using the concrete raw materials of human existence and not in some other, extra-worldly sphere.

It belongs to these convictions that these raw materials of Christian self-realization consist in the whole reality of the world created by God. This, however, makes the task of the Christian one which he does not freely choose himself but which is pre-arranged for him —in short, the concrete existence, the historical hour, into which he is placed. He may and indeed ought to be able to master this task in a different way from the non-Christian. Yet he must fulfil this task and no other. Wherever and whenever one does not want to face up to one's own peculiar situation in one's own particular age but tries instead to take refuge in a world of yesterday—a dreamed-up world, a dead corner of history, a social set-up which was alive and powerful yesterday—one not only falls down on one's earthly task but in such a case Christianity itself suffers both from the artificiality of this existence and the false pretences of the fictitious.

The fact that being a Christian imposes a task within the world does not mean, of course, that "official" Christianity, i.e., the Church herself, must therefore take it into her own hands to develop and advocate a concrete program for an intramundane future derived solely from principles which Christianity alone must advocate. It is impossible to stress that intramundane cultural affairs are relatively autonomous in their own sphere (to stress, indeed, that the Church today must inevitably live in a pluralistic society and cannot under any consideration lay claim to any immediate and direct ruling power in "mundane" matters) *and* at the same time to bemoan the fact that the Church has nothing very clear and stirring to say about the future now dawning and about the way it should be shaped.

But Christians themselves must surrender themselves to the future and regard it as their most proper task, even though this may expose them to uncertainty and risks. Christian lay people, in particular, are not merely organs for carrying out the instructions given by the official hierarchy of the Church, but must themselves try to discover God's unique will for them and for their times.

This again does not mean, however, that the official Church in the most strict sense, i.e., the Church in her own inner life, does not have any tasks arising precisely out of this situation. On the contrary, the Church has many such tasks. She ought to think a lot more about how she can arrange her life and message so as to avoid creating *more* difficulties than are necessary for the man of today and tomorrow—for the men of tomorrow who already live today. The Church is still far from having accomplished this task, and this not only because this task is ever new and must always be solved anew. The Church has also a lot of ground to make up with respect to what she has failed to do in the last one-and-a-half centuries. For during the modern age which is now coming to an end, her thinking and feeling, and her familiarity with the situation, have not kept pace sufficiently with modern developments; during this period she has become more of a conservative power defending herself than was right.

By the fact that she is in arrears with her accomplishment of old tasks, the Church has naturally become overburdened in the fulfilment of her present ones. There are many new tasks for her in Church life and worship, in the reform of the liturgy, in the adaptation of the way of life of the Religious Orders, in the courage to express the old truth in a new way in theology, in the reform of Canon Law. She ought to be reflecting on the problems posed for her by our modern pluralistic world and society, such as the problems arising out of the debate with other religions (or rather, out of the loving attempt to understand them), problems arising in connection with the formation of a type of Christian who can survive and endure the unavoidable and permanent secularization of the world of today, or in connection with the activation of a public influence suited to the society of today and tomorrow.

She should be making her presence felt in this sense through organs which meet the demands of the present and the future, by stirring up courage for planning such as is taking place today (in contrast to previous ages) in all the other dimensions of human existence. She should be presenting the demands of Christian morality in such a way as to make it apparent that they are not incomprehensible imperatives imposed from outside but rather the expression of what is objectively right. She should be establishing a relationship between the clergy and the laity which corresponds to the present condition of lay people and which, while conserving the permanent structure of the Church, does not confuse it with an old-fashioned patriarchism and does not buttress it with taboos about authority which can be safely "demythologized" even within the Church.

If, at the end of these reflections, we now take another look at the brief and formal portrait of the ideology of the future discussed at the beginning, it may be in place here to point out the following: the Christian is completely capable of regarding the planetary unification of world-history under a positively Christian aspect—indeed, from an aspect necessarily demanded by Christianity. In other words, if the universality of the Church is to be or become something real, and is not to be merely something belonging to the basic definition of Christianity, then this can be achieved by Christianity in the concrete only in, together with, and by the creation of this globally unified history.

The Christian will not be surprised to learn, therefore, that this fusion of the history of every nation into one had its real starting point in the very birth of Christianity and in the place where Christianity first took roots in the world and in history, namely in the Western world. If this world of the future is a world of rational planning, a demythologized world, a world secularized by the creature in order that it may serve as the raw material for man's activity, then this whole modern attitude—no matter what particular elements in it we may be able and ought to criticize—is basically a Christian one.

For in the Christian outlook—and only in this outlook—man has become the subject which Western man has discovered himself to be; only in Christianity and by its teaching about the radically created nature of the world as something confided to man to serve as the raw material of *his* activity and as something which is not more important and powerful than man but is meant to serve and is created *for* man, could there spring up that attitude to the cosmos which demythologizes it and which legitimizes the will to control the world. In a metaphysical and theological (Christian) sense, man has always been for Christianity someone who has control over himself and over his own final destiny.

If we consider the doctrine of freedom and of absolute responsibility for self—and the doctrine stating that the particular fate (and eternity) of each individual person is the result of his own free acts—then it becomes clear that the possibility gradually dawning on man today, namely the possibility of making himself the object of his planning and formation, is merely the echo and particular application of that deeper self-responsibility which Christianity has always acknowledged man to possess and which it has always steadfastly refused to relieve him of, since it has always regarded it as his own—sometimes painful—burden.

In the last analysis, therefore, the spirit of the approaching future is not at all as unchristian as the pessimists and the timid often think. Christianity has always been the religion of an infinite future. When Christianity tells us that the future which it professes has always already surpassed all the ideologies concerning the intramundane future of the new man—and when, *even though* in a critical spirit, it examines and tones them down, demythologizing them also, so to speak—then it does this out of a truly Christian, eschatological spirit and not out of a spirit of static conservatism. In this way, Christianity makes man morally responsible to God in his justified desire for an intramundane future—to be created by man himself in unlimited development—and opens this desire to the infinite life of God. This is the life of which it will always remain true (and of which it always becomes true anew) that it has been promised to us as our most proper future by grace.